THE
VISIONARY CEO

MASTERING MINDSET, VISION, AND STRATEGY

JASON MILLER
AND CHRIS O'BYRNE

FOREWORD BY ROBERT RAYMOND,
CEO OF ACHIEVE SYSTEMS

JON HOERAUF, LESLEE COHEN,
JOEL PHILLIPS, MICHAEL SIPE,
PATRICIA BARONOWSKI-SCHNEIDER,
PATRICK LAING, TONY D'URSO,
SHELBY JO LONG, & DR. JULIE DUCHARME

ISBN: 978-1-957217-30-7 (hardback)
ISBN: 978-1-957217-31-4 (paperback)
ISBN: 978-1-957217-32-1 (ebook)

CONTENTS

Foreword

BY
Robert Raymond,
CEO of Achieve Systems

What can you confidently say you have mastered in your own company? It's not a flippant question you just ask at a coffee break or team meeting. It's a weighty question designed to force you to explore your professional skills and knowledge. Rarely do you come across a book that has the power to change not just one aspect but the entire essence of your life and your business. Such a book enriches your intellect and gives you a whole arsenal of extraordinary ideas that catapult you on a path of self-discovery.

It also provides you with actionable insights that you can implement immediately. In our competitive business environment, the ability to quickly grasp content from experts, process it, and then apply it efficiently and effectively is an advantage and the cornerstone of lasting success.

My name is Robert Raymond, CEO of Achieve Systems, one of the largest business-building communities in the world. Our primary mission is closely aligned with my personal passion and lifelong professional focus: Providing entrepreneurs and business owners with a platform to grow, thrive, and achieve unprecedented success in their businesses and lives.

I firmly believe that *The Visionary CEO* is a must-read, and I strongly recommend it. This book is far more than a collection of advice; it is a versatile tool that will help you recalibrate your mindset, develop an unassailable vision that consistently delivers measurable results, and develop a repertoire of actionable strategies. These strategies are designed to fit seamlessly into your existing business model and lifestyle, helping you achieve greater success and satisfaction.

In the grand theater of business, we have all donned several hats and played various roles. We have participated in ventures that have failed spectacularly and basked in the glory of ventures that have been resounding successes. These experiences have been invaluable lessons that smooth the winding path of our professional journey.

This nuanced understanding of the entrepreneurial landscape is precisely embodied in the elite group of CEOs who contributed to this book. They offer a five-star approach that I believe is the gold standard for achieving instant success in the complicated world of business.

One of the most compelling aspects of *The Visionary CEO* is how it brings together Jason Miller and his fellow authors' collective wisdom and life experience. As you move from one chapter to the next, you'll find yourself riveted to your seat and gripped by a sense of anticipation and excitement.

The genius of this book is its unique composition—the combination of high-level professionals bringing their knowledge together to create something extraordinary. The result is an unsurpassed level of content, an unparalleled depth of information, and a carefully crafted roadmap that takes the reader on a journey to personal and professional advancement.

Each author has their own magic, their own unique wisdom that has the potential to be a catalyst for monumental growth in every area of your life. So if you're looking for a business bible that offers more than just tips and tricks, if you're looking for a transformative tool that won't only take you on a journey of self-knowledge but also empower you to take immediate, impactful action, your search is finally over with this book.

As you embark on this journey through the pages of this book, expect to be enlightened, inspired, and most importantly, receive a wealth of actionable insights. Time is a dwindling resource in the business world, and pursuing excellence is a constant, never-ending task. I invite you to take this opportunity to strive for excellence and achieve it. Enjoy the read!

Robert Raymond
CEO of Achieve Systems

CRAFTING A TRANSFORMATIVE VISION: THE CORNERSTONE OF VISIONARY LEADERSHIP

JASON MILLER

In this first book of the three-part series, *The CEO's Path to Excellence*, I address a key aspect of becoming an exceptional leader—developing a transformative vision. Much like a lighthouse guiding a ship, a vision is a CEO's guide through the often-chaotic business world. This chapter highlights this essential component of leadership and draws on the wisdom and experience of seasoned CEOs to give you, the reader, a clear and actionable roadmap.

The visionary CEO is a beacon of innovation and resilience in the rapidly evolving business world, where disruptive technologies and changing consumer behavior are the norm. A compelling vision is the focal point around which this balance revolves. The traditional and visionary paths are no longer separate but pieces of a larger, more complicated puzzle that a CEO must solve. This chapter is an important piece of that puzzle.

My passion is helping companies reach new heights. My journey from combat veteran to executive helping numerous companies grow and succeed has reinforced my belief in the power of a transformative vision. I bring this conviction and a wealth of experience to this chapter.

I have seen how a well-articulated vision can set the direction of a company, create a sense of connection among employees, and drive innovation. However, crafting such a vision is not just about setting goals or developing strategies. It's about understanding your company's purpose and potential and envisioning a future in which both are fulfilled to the highest degree. It's about creating a picture of that future that is so vivid and compelling that your team can't help but put it into action.

But my philosophy goes beyond the confines of the boardroom. I firmly believe that, as CEOs, our visions should also reflect our commitment to positively impacting society. Our companies have the potential to do more than just generate profits; they can touch lives and shape culture. It's up to us as leaders to realize that potential.

In my life, I have committed to continuous learning, which has enriched my understanding of leadership and shaped my approach to developing a transformative vision. I share these insights with you as we explore the invaluable lessons that life brings.

In this chapter, we journey together to discover the art and science of developing a transformative vision. We understand how important it is, how we define it, how we incorporate it into our strategy, and how we communicate it to our teams. I share real-life experiences, both successes and failures, to give you a holistic understanding of what it means to be a visionary CEO.

This chapter is not just an overview; it's a toolbox full of practical wisdom, actionable insights, and proven strategies. It's your first step toward turning your vision into reality, which will propel you to become the visionary CEO your company needs. The future awaits you, so let's start building your transformative vision.

THE NEED FOR A TRANSFORMATIVE VISION

In the business world, where unpredictability reigns and the only constant is change, a transformative vision is an anchor. It is more than a lofty goal or an ambitious dream. I believe it is the lifeblood of an organization, a compass that points all team members in the same direction toward a shared horizon of possibilities.

As a CEO, developing this transformative vision is a great responsibility. I've seen companies with great potential go down in the turmoil of the business world, mainly because they didn't have a compelling vision. On the other hand, I've seen companies rise from irrelevance, not because they had more resources but because they had a vision that transformed them.

What makes this vision so important?

First, a transformative vision is like a lighthouse. In the stormy waters of business, marked by external challenges such as market fluctuations, economic downturns, and changing customer demands, a solid vision ensures that the ship—our company—doesn't drift aimlessly. It provides purpose and direction and ensures all efforts and resources effectively align toward a common goal.

Moreover, a compelling vision is at the heart of innovation. It drives us to challenge the status quo, think outside the box, and imagine a different, better future. When I think of all the revolutionary products, services, and companies that have shaped our world, I don't see them as mere results of hard work, but as expressions of a transformative vision. They came about because someone dared to imagine a world different from the one we live in today.

Moreover, a transformative vision energizes the team. It fosters a shared sense of purpose and creates a bond that transcends the functional boundaries of tasks and hierarchies. When all members of an organization, across all levels of leadership, share in this vision, they become part of something bigger than themselves. This increases motivation and fosters a culture of collaboration, engagement, and resilience.

Perhaps most importantly, a transformative vision is the cornerstone of a CEO's legacy. The vision we communicate will guide and shape the company long after we are gone. It is our most lasting contribution, the mark we leave behind. This realization lends exceptional gravity to the task and makes it imperative that we develop a vision that is not only ambitious but also holistic, sustainable, and inclusive.

In my journey as a leader and lifelong learner, I have learned that, while important, strategies, tactics, and operational excellence are only one vessel. What animates these vessels and gives them direction and meaning is transformative vision. Without it, even the most efficient vessel will merely drift aimlessly.

As CEOs, we have the privilege and challenge of steering our organizations into the future. A transformative vision is our strongest ally, providing clarity in the face of uncertainty and inspiration in difficult times. Developing and sustaining this vision is necessary and essential to survive and thrive in the dynamic business world.

Defining Your Vision

Designing a vision isn't about predicting the future with pinpoint accuracy. Instead, it's about creating a roadmap focusing on your organization's highest goals and values. It's both an end goal and an ongoing journey that continues to be refined through new insights and experiences. Every leader takes their own path to crystallize their vision, but here are some steps that have served me well and may be instructive for you as well.

1. **Reflection:** Start by looking inward. Ask yourself, *What is the core purpose of my company? Why doesn't it exist just to make a profit?* For some, it may be about driving innovation; for others, it's about enriching the community or championing sustainability. This intrinsic motivation becomes the core of your vision.

2. **Think ahead:** Imagine where your company will be in five, ten, or even twenty years. While the details may still be unclear, the broad strokes—like the impact you want to have on society or the legacy you want to leave behind—should come into focus.

3. **Align with values:** Ensure your vision aligns with your organization's core values. A mismatch between what you want to achieve and the values you hold will cause friction and disagreement.

4. **Consult your team:** The best visions often come from collaboration. Talk to your leadership team, your employees, and your customers. Their feedback can provide valuable perspective and refine your vision, making it more holistic and grounded.

5. **Make it tangible:** A vision should inspire and be somewhat tangible. You should strike a balance between what you want and what you can achieve. It should

challenge your organization but not be so far-fetched it becomes demotivating.

6. **Communicate and engage:** Once your vision is created, it needs to be communicated throughout the organization and integrated into the structure of the organization. It should be the basis for decision-making at all levels and reviewed regularly to ensure alignment and relevance.

To illustrate, I'd like to explain the development of the vision for the Strategic Advisor Board (SAB). When I launched SAB, it wasn't just about providing consulting services. It was about filling knowledge gaps and promoting the growth of small and medium-sized businesses, which I believe are the backbone of our economy.

As I thought about it, I realized my passion was to create a collaborative ecosystem that would bring together expertise from different industries and provide unparalleled strategic insights to companies. I envisioned SAB as both a consulting firm and a knowledge hub.

The core values of collaboration, empowerment, and knowledge-based growth became pillars that supported our vision. As I discussed this with our team of CEO advisors, it was further refined. Their diverse experiences brought nuance and emphasized finding solutions tailored to each company's unique challenges.

The tangible aspect of our vision was the measurable growth our clients would achieve through increased sales, expansion into new markets or innovative product launches. Every strategy, every consultation, and every investment SAB makes is driven by this vision.

Today, our vision for SAB is: "We help companies achieve unprecedented growth, innovation, and sustainable success through shared expertise."

This is our North Star guiding all our decisions and actions. It inspires our team and gives our clients clarity on what to expect when they work with us.

While defining a vision can be introspective and intense, its clarity and direction make it an invaluable part of a CEO's toolbox. Your vision is your legacy. Craft it with care.

EMBEDDING THE VISION

Anchoring a vision in an organization is much like planting a seed and nurturing it to grow. Having a vision isn't enough. For it to truly take root and bear fruit, it must be interwoven with all levels of the organization, from culture to strategy. This ensures that the vision isn't just a statement on the wall, but a living, breathing ethos that influences actions and decisions.

1. **Communicate clearly:** First and foremost, make sure everyone in the organization—from top management to employees—understands the vision. This can take the form of meetings, workshops, or communication campaigns. The medium may vary, but the goal remains the same: Every individual should be able to articulate the vision and understand its meaning.

2. **Leadership alignment:** Leaders within the organization must be the torchbearers of the vision. Their actions, decisions, and communications should reflect and reinforce the vision at every opportunity. Regular training and alignment meetings with leaders can help achieve this.

3. **Commit to the strategy:** As you develop strategic goals, you need to make sure they align with the vision. This means that every new product, service, and market expansion should align with the core of the vision.

4. **Celebrate successes that align with the vision:** Recognize and reward actions and results that align particularly well with the vision. This not only underscores the importance of the vision but also encourages behaviors that bring the vision to life.

5. **Regular reviews:** Like any strategic component, the anchoring of a vision should be reviewed regularly. This ensures that the organization stays on track and that deviations are corrected promptly.

6. **Foster a culture of ownership:** Empower every member of the organization to take ownership of the vision. This fosters a sense of collective ownership and ensures that the vision isn't imposed from above but is shared by all.

In my journey with the Strategic Advisor Board (SAB), realizing our vision to "help organizations achieve unprecedented growth, innovation, and sustainable success through shared expertise" has been challenging and rewarding.

First, I spent a great deal of time with our leadership team discussing the finer points of the vision. We debated, refined, and eventually agreed on the vision for each department, such as sales, marketing, or operations. This detailed understanding was critical because it formed the basis for later decisions and strategies.

We also made sure that our interactions with our customers were always consistent with our vision. This meant that we offered them solutions and ensured that those solutions were co-developed and tailored for growth and innovation. Our success stories, such as one customer's 300% increase in revenue within ninety days, were celebrated across the company and illustrated the impact of our vision.

In our quarterly reviews, we included a section on the alignment of our vision in addition to standard metrics and KPIs. This served as a regular checkpoint that ensured we stayed on track.

This effort resulted in a cohesive, aligned organization where the vision wasn't just words but a tangible force that drove every action. The alignment between our vision and day-to-day operations became so seamless that customers, partners, and even new employees could feel and articulate it.

Embedding a vision is about making it the heart and soul of your business. That takes consistent effort, adjustment, and reinforcement, but the results—a motivated team, clear direction, and sustainable growth—are worth the effort.

COMMUNICATING THE VISION

No matter how profound and transformative, a vision remains only a lofty goal if it's not communicated effectively. Communication is critical to breathe life into a vision and turning it from abstract to actionable. It's the bridge between aspiration and realization, the medium that transforms intention into collective momentum.

Think of the vision as the North Star. It shines brightly in the night sky, guiding sailors and explorers alike, but its value depends on people knowing where to look, understanding its meaning, and believing in its permanence. For the corporate vision to serve its purpose, it must be visible, understood, and trusted by everyone in the company.

1. **Clarity is key:** The vision should be articulated in an inspiring and clear way. Avoid jargon or overly complex language. The goal is that everyone, regardless of position or background, can understand it effortlessly. When crafting the message, ask yourself, "Could anyone in any department explain this to me?"

2. **Repetition makes you strong:** Consistency is the cornerstone of effective communication. A vision isn't something you say once and then forget. It should be repeated regularly—in town halls, team meetings, internal newsletters, and even casual conversations. Repetition reinforces the vision and signals its importance to the organization.

3. **Include multiple channels:** In today's diverse and digital workplace, it's important to use multiple communication channels. From intranet posts and email campaigns to webinars and interactive workshops, cast a wide net to ensure the message reaches everyone.

4. **Leadership as a beacon:** Leaders play a central role in communicating the vision. Their actions, words, and decisions should consistently reflect the vision. When the workforce sees their leaders embody the vision, it increases credibility and builds trust.

5. **Encourage dialogs, not monologs:** Encourage discussions about the vision. Create forums where employees can share their interpretations, ask questions, or challenge aspects. This two-way communication provides a better understanding and fosters a sense of ownership and engagement.

6. **Integrate it into onboarding:** It's just as important for new employees to understand the company's vision as it's to know their job responsibilities. Integrate communication of the vision into the onboarding process

and ensure they begin their journey with a clear sense of direction.

7. **Celebrate alignment:** Recognize and praise when teams or individuals exemplify the vision through their actions or results. Not only is this motivating, but it's also a practical example of how the vision is put into action.

Every time I think about the importance of communicating a vision, I can't help but think of an example from my early days as an entrepreneur. We had developed what I thought was a compelling vision for our fledgling company. However, a few months later, at a team meeting, I was astonished to discover that only a fraction of our team could articulate our vision correctly. This wasn't because of them but because of me. I had assumed that a few emails and an introductory meeting would suffice. I couldn't have been more wrong.

A concerted effort followed to incorporate the vision into our daily work. We began our meetings with a summary of the vision, developed interactive modules to understand and interpret the vision, and most importantly, created an environment where the vision was lived, not just talked about.

The change was palpable. Decisions were made faster, teams were more aligned, and the overall mood improved. It was a powerful lesson in the transformative power of effectively communicating a vision.

A vision guides and points the way to the future. However, it must be communicated consistently and persuasively to fulfill this vital role. Only then can it spur an organization to unified, goal-oriented action.

Nurturing a Visionary Culture

Culture, often referred to as the lifeblood of an organization, is a complex web of values, beliefs, behaviors, and norms that shape the nature of the organization. Even as strategies and goals change, culture remains the unshakable pillar that guides those changes. For a vision to truly thrive, it must be rooted in the fertile soil of an aligned culture. A visionary culture supports, promotes, and drives an organization's overarching vision.

However, developing such a culture isn't a matter of mere proclamation. It's a deliberate and ongoing effort that weaves together various elements to create an environment where the vision isn't only respected but revered. Here's a guide on how to cultivate a visionary culture:

1. **Lead by example:** As leaders, our actions speak louder than our words. If we want our teams to embrace and commit to a vision, we must first embody it ourselves. This includes making decisions that align with the vision, speaking passionately about it, and modeling behaviors that align with it. When teams see this congruence in their leadership, they're more likely to follow it.

2. **Participate in creating the vision:** Even if only a few articulate the vision, it's intended for the many. Involve different levels of the organization in refining or redefining the vision. If each individual feels they have contributed to its creation, they'll participate more fully in its implementation.

3. **Continuous learning:** Foster a culture of learning and growing. Host workshops, seminars, and training sessions that emphasize the importance of visionary thinking. Not only will this equip teams with the skills they need, but it'll also highlight the importance the company places on forward-thinking.

4. **Reward visionary behavior:** What gets rewarded gets repeated. Appreciate and celebrate actions, initiatives, or results that align with the company's vision. This can include monthly awards, public recognition, or even material incentives.

5. **Open communication channels:** Encourage open dialog about the vision. Create platforms where employees can voice their opinions, ask questions, or share ideas about the vision. This creates clarity and fosters a sense of ownership and belonging.

6. **A collaborative environment:** A vision is a collective dream. Create an environment that fosters collaboration, where departments, teams, and individuals work toward a common goal. This collaborative spirit reinforces the collective nature of the vision.

7. **Review the vision regularly:** The business world is dynamic, and even if the core of the vision remains constant, its wording may need to be adjusted. Periodic reviews of the vision ensure that it remains relevant and resonates.

Fostering a visionary culture is about creating an environment where vision is the heartbeat that is felt and echoed in every corridor, cubicle, and conference room. It's about fostering pride in the vision and ensuring every member feels part of something bigger and profound. When this culture is successfully cultivated, the vision transforms from an organizational goal into a personal mission everyone is passionate about.

Embracing Continuous Learning

In a world of rapid technological advancement, changing consumer behavior, and ever-changing market dynamics, resting on past successes is a recipe for stagnation. Visionary leadership requires more than looking to the horizon; it must understand the terrain, recognize new patterns, and adapt to new realities. At the heart of this adaptability is the principle of continuous learning.

Leading with vision means accepting our knowledge is not finite and today's best practices may become obsolete tomorrow. It means recognizing that our education does not end with a diploma or a certificate but is a lifelong journey. Therefore, continuous learning is the essence of visionary leadership:

1. **Staying ahead of the curve:** Markets evolve, technologies change, and what is considered innovative today may be commonplace tomorrow. Continuous learning enables leaders to keep pace with these changes and ensure their strategies are relevant and groundbreaking. It's about anticipating change rather than just reacting to it.

2. **Cultivate a growth mindset:** Carol Dweck's seminal work described the difference between fixed and growth mindsets. Leaders with a growth mindset, fueled by continuous learning, believe in their ability to evolve and grow. This mindset is contagious and creates organizations that are resilient, adaptive, and growth oriented.

3. **Enriching decision-making:** Our decisions are only as good as the information we base them on. By constantly updating our knowledge, we enrich our perspectives, leading to better-informed, holistic, and strategic decisions.

4. **Fostering innovation:** Innovation is not a sudden eureka moment but the result of diverse experiences, knowledge, and insights. A commitment to continuous learning fosters an environment where new ideas are desired and inevitable.

5. **Build authentic leadership:** Leaders who invest in learning show vulnerability—they admit they don't know all the answers. This authenticity builds trust, makes teams more receptive to leadership, and makes them more responsive to the leader's vision.

Recognizing the importance of continuous learning is one aspect; integrating it into your routine is another. Here are some practical ways leaders can internalize this philosophy:

Take time to learn: Schedule time in your weekly schedule for learning. This could be reading articles, attending webinars, or listening to podcasts.

Educate yourself formally: Consider courses, certifications, or even advanced degrees that can improve your expertise in your field or areas where you feel a gap.

Attend workshops and conferences: Such platforms offer a double benefit: Gaining knowledge and expanding your network.

Encourage team learning: create platforms for members to share insights, articles, or learning resources. When an entire team values learning, a collective growth dynamic is created.

Be curious: Ask questions, inquire about other opinions, and challenge your own assumptions. Curiosity is the precursor to learning.

In my journey with the Strategic Advisor Board, I've made it a ritual to dedicate the first hour of my day to learning. Whether understanding a new market trend, exploring a new management philosophy, or simply exploring an area unrelated to my industry, this habit is my compass as I navigate the uncertain waters of business management. It has enriched my strategies and created a culture in my company where learning is valued, discussions are lively, and innovation is organic.

Visionary leadership is not about having a crystal ball that predicts the future. It's about constantly refining the lens through which you view the future; constant learning is that clean lens. Embrace it, commit to it, and watch your vision become sharper, clearer, and more tangible.

MAINTAINING THE VISION THROUGH CHALLENGES

No matter how experienced or successful, every visionary leader will experience moments when their zeal is tested. These are the challenging times when the market is unpredictable, competition is fierce, or internal conflicts arise. At such moments, it's not uncommon for the vision that once seemed so clear and achievable to be challenged. But at such moments, a clearly defined vision proves to be the beacon that guides companies through stormy waters.

The role of vision in difficult times cannot be overstated. Here's why:

1. **A vision provides stability:** When external factors seem overwhelming, a clear vision is the cornerstone of stability. It reminds everyone in the organization of the "why" behind their actions. Just as ships use lighthouses to navigate stormy waters, organizations use their vision to navigate uncertain times.

2. **Promotes resilience:** Difficulties are inevitable, but how we respond to them determines our path. A strong vision strengthens resilience. It conveys the belief that current challenges are only temporary obstacles on the path to a greater goal. When the entire organization

believes in a shared vision, collective resilience grows many times over.

3. **Prevents reactive decision-making:** In the face of challenges, there is often a temptation to make hasty decisions for a quick fix. A clear vision ensures that all decisions, even if made in the heat of the moment, are consistent with long-term goals. It prevents detours and ensures that short-term reactions don't jeopardize long-term success.

4. **Encourages innovation:** Ironically, challenges, when viewed through the lens of vision, can become catalysts for innovation. They force organizations to think differently and find new solutions. A clear vision provides a framework for this innovation and ensures that new ideas not only address the immediate challenges but also align with the organization's larger goals.

5. **Fosters unity:** A shared vision is the glue that holds teams together during difficult times. When individuals have differing opinions about addressing challenges, the vision serves as common ground, a unifying force that aligns efforts and energies.

During my years as a leader in my many businesses, there were several moments when our resolve was tested. There was a time when market dynamics changed so rapidly that many of our proven strategies became obsolete overnight. Doubts arose, both in my mind and in the team. But our vision—to provide companies with unparalleled strategic advice and solutions—wouldn't let go.

Instead of seeing market changes as insurmountable challenges, our vision helped us see them as opportunities. We reviewed our strategies, realigned our goals, and renewed our approaches. The challenges didn't get smaller, but our perspective changed, thanks to our vision.

Whenever we encountered an obstacle, we asked ourselves, "Is our approach consistent with our vision?" Despite the adversity, this simple question became our touchstone and ensured that we never lost sight of our overarching goal.

Leaders need to understand that, while challenges are scary, they're also opportunities. They allow us to rethink our vision to ensure it's relevant and resilient. Leaders must communicate the vision and embody it, live it, and use it as an incentive. For visionary leaders, challenges aren't setbacks but the foundation for greater success guided by a steadfast vision amid adversity.

KEY TAKEAWAYS FROM THIS CHAPTER

To conclude this chapter, let me summarize the key insights that can reshape how we perceive and implement visionary leadership.

1. **The importance of vision:** A clear, compelling, and transformative vision is at the heart of visionary leadership. It's more than a mission statement or a corporate goal. The bigger picture, the larger goal, and the dream drive an organization. Without a transformative vision, leadership becomes reactive, transient, and aimless.

2. **Define the vision:** A vision doesn't appear out of thin air. It's the result of introspection, market intelligence, and foresight. It requires clear thinking and goal setting. Visionary leaders take time to define their vision and ensure that it aligns with their personal values and their company's long-term goals.

3. **Anchoring the vision:** Once a vision is articulated, it must be integrated into the organization's fabric. It should drive strategy, guide decision-making, and influence the organization's culture. A vision that remains isolated from day-to-day operations is mere rhetoric.

Visionary leaders ensure that their vision is alive, tangible, and actionable in every aspect of their business.

4. **Communicate with clarity:** No matter how grand, a vision is useless if it's not communicated effectively. Leaders' responsibility is to ensure that everyone involved—from top management to lower levels of the workforce—understands the vision and feels personally connected to it. Communication isn't a one-time affair but an ongoing process of reinforcement.

5. **Cultivate a visionary culture:** A vision is only as strong as a shared belief in it. Leaders must foster a culture where the vision is celebrated, employees are encouraged to align their tasks with the overarching vision, and everyone has a common goal in mind.

6. **Encourage continuous learning:** The business world is constantly changing. What is current today may be obsolete tomorrow. Visionary leaders remain adaptable and agile, fostering a culture of continuous learning. They stay current, encourage their teams to continue their education, and ensure that their vision evolves with the dynamics of change.

7. **Resilience in the face of adversity:** Challenges are a given. But vision is the compass in these difficult times. It fosters resilience, guides decision-making, and ensures short-term setbacks don't derail long-term goals.

In this chapter, I have discussed the principles I learned in theory and experienced in practice, particularly through my experiences as CEO of the Strategic Advisor Board. The trials, triumphs, and changes we have gone through are a testament to the power of visionary leadership.

Being a visionary leader is a journey, not a destination. It requires constant development, unwavering commitment, and the ability to think outside the box. It's about dreaming big but anchoring those dreams in actionable strategies. It's about inspiring teams, overcoming challenges, and always considering the big picture.

Throughout the rest of this book, I ask you to keep these insights in mind, internalize them, and consider how to apply them to your leadership career. In the business world, it's the visionaries who leave indelible marks and shape their companies—and the future of the industry.

ABOUT THE AUTHOR

Jason Founded the Strategic Advisor Board in 2017 and became the Senior Global Council Member (CEO and Chairman of the Board) upon its inception. He holds multiple chair roles in other companies to include several non-profits. Jason's major strengths are in Hyper Company Growth, Scaling, Deal Flow Management, and Strategic & Operational implementation. Jason has built over twenty-four companies from the ground up since 2001.

As the CEO, Jason has been charged with overseeing the growth of the Strategic Advisor Board and the oversight of the team and its capabilities as a core business globally. His primary focus is to maintain a positive company culture which allows its partners and council members to thrive in their duties while serving SAB clients across the globe.

Jason has increased his focus and impact around creating sustainable business models for companies of all sizes with a focus on leadership responsibility, accountability and Diversity, Equity, Inclusion, and Accessibility, which he literally wrote the book on. As a veteran himself, Jason has committed to serving as many veteran-owned companies as possible and has committed to a five-year plan of pro bono work for veteran organizations that need help.

Throughout his over thirty years of experience, Jason has advised thousands of leaders from around the globe and has been recognized as being one of the foremost leaders in the consulting world for creating scalable business models for small and mid-market companies. He is known for big ideas and creating large scale transformations for organizations and was nicknamed Jason "The Bull" Miller as he has a no-excuses approach to clients executing on the strategies that the Global Council Members provide.

He is a sitting chairman of the American Club Association, Board of Directors for the Leigh Steinberg Academy, Forbes Council, Entrepreneur Magazine Leadership council and many other organizations that impact business globally. He is a lifetime member of the American Legion, Disabled American Veterans (DAV) and Veterans of Foreign Wars (VFW).

Jason Holds an MBA from Trident University and a PhD from the school of hard knocks. He continues to learn and grow as a leader himself to provide the best workplace for his teams and business strategies for their clients. Jason lives in Boulder, Colorado with his wife and two children. Jason has two that are out of the house and three grand babies.

Leading by Influence

Chris O'Byrne

"Leading by Influence" presents a unique perspective on leadership that goes beyond the traditional focus on authority or power and emphasizes the ability to inspire and lead others. Influence, in this framework, is described as the ability to influence the behavior and thinking of others to achieve a shared vision.

Traditional leadership styles are often based on formal titles, hierarchical superiority, or the mere exercise of power. In contrast, the role of the visionary CEO or influential leader is to inspire and motivate their teams to achieve their vision. This approach is less about commanding and more about showing the path to success, igniting enthusiasm, and encouraging individuals to strive for their highest potential.

A visionary CEO or influential leader is characterized by strong relationships, proven expertise, effective communication, and their status as a role model. These leaders exude authenticity and the highest integrity and earn respect through their actions, not just their titles.

The linchpin of such an influential leader is a powerful and transformative message—a vision—that resonates strongly with others. This vision shapes the essence of your leadership, influences your actions, and guides your decision-making processes. The clarity and credibility of your vision is directly proportional to the breadth and depth of your influence.

This chapter explores transitioning from a traditional leader to a visionary CEO or influential leader. We will explore the reasons for this transition, the characteristics of such a leader, and the strategies for increasing your influence to benefit your team and organization.

Before we become influential leaders, it's essential to understand why this goal is so important. What drives us to gain influence and break out of ignorance? The "why" of becoming an influential leader lies in our desire to have a profound and positive impact on the people we lead and our broader sphere of influence.

First, influence helps us formulate our unique message as a leader. A leader's message is their vision, ethos, and promise. It summarizes what they stand for and what they want to achieve. Every leader has a unique message, something they want to be known for. But having a message is not enough. It must also be communicated effectively and, most importantly, resonate with others. An influential leader can deliver a message that inspires, motivates, and potentially changes the lives of her followers. It is this transformative potential that defines many influential leaders.

Second, becoming an influential leader requires stepping into the spotlight rather than hiding. Every leader starts somewhere, often in a relatively unknown place. On the path to becoming an influential leader, you must amplify your voice, refine your message, and improve your leadership style. As your influence grows, so does your ability to effect change, make a difference, and lead your team toward common goals. This development and growth process is another compelling reason why many choose the path of influential leadership.

Finally, the influence of a leader has a domino effect. An influential leader's influence extends beyond their immediate team and impacts their company, industry, and community. The potential to have more power is an enticing "why" for many leaders. The more influence you have, the greater your ability to effect positive change on a larger scale. This is especially true for servant leaders, who lead by serving others. Your influence can foster a culture of mutual respect, trust, and collaboration, creating a more harmonious and productive work environment.

In summary, the 'why' to become an influential leader revolves around the desire to articulate a strong message, step out of the shadows and effect positive change. It's about seizing the opportunity to make a difference in the lives of others and using influence as a tool. The power of influence in leadership can bring about change for the leader themselves and the people they lead.

DEFINITION OF INFLUENCE IN THE CONTEXT OF LEADERSHIP

Influence in the context of leadership goes far beyond the mere power to control or command. Influence isn't about forcing obedience through authority but inspiring others to willingly follow and give their best to achieve a common goal. It's about the ability to shape, direct, and influence the development or behavior of others through indirect or intangible means.

At the heart of influence is the art of persuasion. Influential leaders are persuasive leaders. They can articulate their visions and values in a way that resonates with others. They can make compelling arguments for their strategies and decisions and help others understand the "why" behind their actions.

Influential leadership also means establishing credibility. Influential leaders have demonstrated that they're trustworthy and dependable. They have demonstrated competence, integrity, and consistency, inspiring trust and respect among their followers. This trust and respect gives these leaders the social capital to influence the thoughts and actions of others.

In addition, influential leadership is about building relationships. Influential leaders cultivate close relationships with the people they lead, fostering a sense of mutual respect and understanding. They listen to their team, value their contributions, and create an environment where everyone feels heard and valued. This relationship-based approach makes it more likely that others will support the leader's vision and course.

Part of being an influential leader is the ability to inspire. Influential leaders are inspirational leaders. They can ignite enthusiasm, spark passion, and inspire others to think innovatively. They motivate their team not by dictation but by their example of commitment, resilience, and dedication to the shared vision.

Influence in the context of leadership is a multi-layered mix of conviction, credibility, relationship building, and inspiration. It's the ability to lead, shape, and inspire others toward a shared vision or goal and create an environment where every team member feels motivated to do their best.

NUMBER OF PEOPLE INFLUENCED

The number of people influenced determines a leader's reach and influence. It measures the breadth of a leader's impact and indicates how widely their message, vision, or direction is spread and accepted.

One might ask why the number of people influenced is essential. Isn't the quality of influence more important than the number of people influenced? While it's true that the depth or quality of influence on a person is significant, the number of people who are influenced has a value all its own in the realm of leadership.

The number of people a leader influences is a testament to their ability to communicate effectively with everyone. This ability is crucial in large organizations, public administration, and any situation where the leader's decisions and actions have far-reaching implications. Leaders who successfully communicate their vision and values to large audiences can effect significant change, gain support, and foster collective action toward common goals.

In addition, the number of people influencing a leader's message can amplify their impact. The more people who support a leader's vision, the stronger that vision becomes. This collective belief can accelerate progress toward goals, boost morale, and create a shared purpose within a group, organization, or community.

When a leader has the backing of a large group, it not only validates their leadership skills but also strengthens their position and makes it easier for them to overcome challenges, overcome resistance, and effect change.

Leaders should remember, however, that while quantity is important, it should never come at the expense of quality. True leadership is about effecting meaningful change and inspiring others to do their best. It's about finding the right balance between the number of people you reach and the depth of impact you have on each person.

QUALITY OF THE LEADER'S MESSAGE

A leader's message serves as a guide, a compass that leads an organization or team toward its common goals. The quality of this message is, therefore, of paramount importance. It determines what the leader stands for and sets the tone for the culture, values, and vision of the entire organization or team.

At the heart of a good leadership message is clarity. A leader's message must be clear, concise, and easy to understand. It must succinctly convey the leader's vision and the strategic direction they want to take. Clarity promotes understanding and helps ensure everyone is on the same page and working toward the same goals.

Closely related to clarity is consistency. The quality of a leader's message is strengthened when it is consistent, both over time and across different platforms or contexts. Consistency builds trust and reliability and helps create a solid and recognizable leadership brand.

The quality of a leader's message is also determined by its relevance. A compelling message is focused on the target audience and addresses their needs, desires, and concerns. A leader should know the pulse of their team or organization and craft their message to be inspiring, motivating, and effective.

Moreover, their authenticity enhances the quality of a leader's message. Authentic messages truly reflect the leader's beliefs, values, and vision. When a leader's message is authentic, it is more likely to inspire trust, loyalty, and commitment in their followers.

Finally, the quality of a leader's message also depends on their transformational potential. The best leadership messages can inspire change, drive innovation, and stimulate growth. They are visionary, push boundaries, and challenge the status quo.

They inspire their followers to strive for better, go beyond their comfort zone, and work to achieve their vision.

The quality of a leader's message is determined by its clarity, consistency, relevance, authenticity, and transformative potential. A high-quality message can be a powerful tool in a leader's arsenal that significantly increases their influence and impact.

THE IMPORTANCE OF IDENTIFYING YOUR UNIQUE MESSAGE AS A LEADER

Identifying your unique message as a leader is essential to effective leadership. Your leadership signature—the unique blend of your values, vision, and purpose—sets you apart. Here's why it's so important:

1. **Authenticity.** Your unique message expresses your authentic self. It reflects your values, beliefs, experiences, and perspectives. Authenticity builds trust and credibility. When your team sees that your leadership message is consistent with who you're and how you behave, they're more likely to trust and follow you.

2. **Differentiation.** Your unique message helps you stand out in a world with many leaders. It sets you apart from others and gives your team or organization an excellent reason to follow you. This differentiator can be a crucial advantage in a crowded leadership environment, helping you gain support and inspire loyalty.

3. **Inspiration.** A unique message often has a personal and passionate touch that generic messages lack. This personal connection to your message can make it more inspiring and motivating to your team. They're not just working for any cause but a cause you deeply believe in and are passionate about.

4. **Direction.** Your unique leadership message provides a clear direction for your team or organization. It outlines your vision for the future and guides decision-making and strategy. This clarity of purpose helps ensure everyone is working toward the same goals.

5. **Connection.** When you lead with a message that is truly your own, others can get to know and understand you better. This fosters a deeper connection with your team or organization and improves collaboration, communication, and mutual understanding.

6. **Influence.** Your unique message can increase your influence as a leader. It can make your voice more memorable and your vision more compelling. When your message is clear and concise, it's more likely to be listened to, remembered, and acted upon.

Finding your unique leadership message is critical. It's about authenticity, differentiation, inspiration, direction, connection, and influence. When you focus on what you want to be known for as a leader, you can effectively lead, inspire, and influence your team or organization to shared success.

WHAT DO YOU WANT TO BE KNOWN FOR?

As a leader, figuring out what you want to be known for is tantamount to determining your leadership legacy. This is a critical step because it forms the foundation of your leadership ethos and shapes your unique message to your team, organization, or even the world. Here are a few key areas you should consider.

1. **Values.** What are the core values that drive you? Integrity, authenticity, empathy, resilience, and optimism are just a few examples. When you know these values, you can embody them in your leadership style,

actions, and decisions and make them an essential part of your legacy.

2. **Vision.** What is your vision for your team, company, or industry? Do you want to drive innovation, foster a positive culture, revolutionize customer service, or champion social responsibility? Your vision can be an essential part of your leadership identity.

3. **Skills and expertise.** Are there specific skills or areas of expertise you want to be recognized for? Perhaps you're an exceptional strategic thinker, an effective communicator, a digital transformation guru, or a team-building expert. These strengths can help define your leadership brand.

4. **Impact.** What impact do you want to have on your team, organization, or community? Do you want to inspire personal growth, drive business success, or contribute to social change? Figuring out what you want to impact will help you set the direction for your leadership.

5. **Style.** What kind of leader do you want to be? Do you want to be known as a transformational leader who inspires and motivates, a servant leader who puts the team's needs first, or a democratic leader who encourages participation and consensus? Your leadership style can significantly impact how you're perceived and remembered.

Thinking about these areas can help you determine what you want to be known for as a leader. Remember that your legacy as a leader isn't just about your accomplishments or successes but also about the values you espouse, the vision you champion, the expertise you bring, the impact you make, and the unique leadership style you embody.

HOW YOUR MESSAGE CAN CHANGE LIVES

As a leader, your message has remarkable potential for change. The right words, delivered with conviction and sincerity, can inspire, motivate, and lead others to meaningful change. Here's how your message can change lives:

1. **Inspire Action.** A compelling message can inspire people to take action. It can be a call to tackle a complex problem, strive for an important goal, or make a significant change. By articulating your vision in a way that resonates with others, you can move them from inertia to action.

2. **Change perspective.** Your message can help others see things differently or challenge existing assumptions. A transformative message often encourages critical thinking and opens up new ways of understanding the world, helping people broaden their perspectives.

3. **Build self-confidence.** As a leader, your message can build and strengthen your team's confidence or following. Conveying belief in your team's abilities and recognizing their accomplishments can boost their self-esteem and encourage them to take on more significant challenges.

4. **Promote resilience.** Your message can help foster resilience in adversity. By conveying hope, perseverance, and the value of learning from failure, you can encourage others to persevere through difficult times.

5. **Promote growth and development.** A strong leadership message often promotes personal and professional growth. It may encourage continuous learning, stimulate creativity, or emphasize the importance of feedback and improvement. This can lead people to develop new skills, gain new insights, and advance their careers.

6. **Build community.** Your message can also help foster a sense of community and belonging. By highlighting shared values, common goals, and mutual support, you can strengthen social bonds and create a culture of collaboration and inclusion.

Your message as a leader has the potential to create change that goes far beyond the immediate context and profoundly impacts the lives of those you lead. That's why it's important to be aware of the impact of your words and carefully craft and deliver your message to inspire and promote change.

THE WAY FROM OBSCURITY TO INFLUENCE

The journey from obscurity to influence is a transformative process that requires strategic action, continuous learning, and authentic engagement. Here's one possible roadmap.

1. **Clarify your message.** As mentioned earlier, it's essential to be clear about your unique message as a leader. What values, vision, and impact do you want to associate with your leadership role? What do you want to be known for? A clear, authentic, and compelling message is the foundation of your influence.

2. **Develop your skills and expertise.** You must be more than just a figurehead. Being knowledgeable in your field is essential if you wish to gain respect and authority. Take the time to learn, improve and become a thought leader in your field. Your credibility and expertise will naturally attract followers.

3. **Build your network.** Influence is often the result of a solid and diverse network. Start by strengthening the relationships in your immediate area and then gradually expand your sphere of influence. Attend industry events, participate in online forums, and

engage in community projects. Remember that real connections breed the most influential relationships.

4. **Use platforms to amplify your voice.** In today's connected world, multiple platforms can help amplify your voice. Start a blog, write a book, run a podcast, use social media, or speak at public events. These platforms allow you to share your insights, connect with your audience, and establish your thought leadership.

5. **Create value for others.** The most influential leaders add value to others. Whether you're sharing knowledge, offering solutions, inspiring action, or simply offering support: When people notice you positively contributing to their lives, your influence grows naturally.

6. **Be consistent and persistent.** Building influence takes time. Stay consistent in your message, values, and actions. Even with setbacks or slow progress, persistence is key.

7. **Seek feedback and constantly improve.** Influence isn't a static end goal but a dynamic process. Seek feedback, learn from your experiences, and continuously adapt and improve. Your influence will increase over time as you respond to change and show your commitment to growth.

The journey from obscurity to influence isn't about gaining fame or power but strengthening your ability to effect change, inspire others, and make a meaningful difference. Remember that the greatest influence isn't wielded through authority or coercion but is earned through respect, trust, and shared values.

Rethink your motivations for your pursuit of influence

An essential aspect of leadership is understanding your motivations for your pursuit of influence. Influence is essentially the ability to influence outcomes and inspire others. The desire to influence can arise from various motives, sometimes noble and sometimes self-serving. As a leader, it's important to think about your intentions. Here are some points to keep in mind.

1. **Make a difference.** If your motivation to make a difference is to bring about positive change in your company, industry, or the world, that's a sign of a servant leader. You focus on the common good and use your influence to shape policy, practice, and culture in ways that contribute to a better future.

2. **Personal development.** Motivation lies in personal development and fulfillment for some people. The challenge of leading, the satisfaction of achieving goals, and the opportunity to leave a lasting legacy can be powerful drivers for you.

3. **Recognition and respect.** Some leaders seek influence to gain recognition and respect from colleagues, employees, and society. While this isn't necessarily negative, it's important that your pursuit of respect doesn't overshadow the needs of those you lead.

4. **Power and control.** You must be careful if your primary motivation is to gain power or control over others. Influence based on power alone can lead to authoritarianism and create a culture of fear rather than inspiration.

Reflecting on your motivations for seeking influence isn't a one-time task. On your journey to becoming a leader, your motivations may change. Regular self-reflection can help you stay aligned with your values, ensure you're using your power responsibly, and improve your ability to lead with empathy and authenticity.

Remember that the best leaders don't wield their influence for power's sake but to empower others, foster growth, and drive positive change.

THE POWER AND INFLUENCE OF AN INFLUENTIAL LEADER

An influential leader has a lot of power and can greatly influence individuals and organizations. The following is about the 'what"—the power and influence that such a leader can wield:

1. **Driving vision and strategy.** An influential leader can effectively communicate and drive an organization's vision and strategy. They can pull their team along and ensure that everyone is working towards a common goal, increasing the organization's overall performance.

2. **Inspire and motivate others.** Influential leaders can inspire and motivate their team members. Their energy, vision, and belief in each individual's potential can create a positive work environment, increase productivity, and foster a sense of ownership among team members.

3. **They create a positive organizational culture.** Through their actions, attitudes, and behaviors, influential leaders can shape the culture of their organization. They can create an environment of trust, collaboration, innovation, and continuous learning, leading to higher employee engagement and satisfaction.

4. **Influencing change.** Influential leaders have the power to drive change. They can challenge the status quo, encourage innovation, and lead their teams through times of change. They can also influence overall industry trends and standards.

5. **Build strong networks.** Influential leaders can build and maintain strong networks inside and outside their

organizations. These networks can be leveraged for collaboration to gain new insights and create more opportunities for the organization.

6. **Mentoring and developing others.** Influential leaders often act as mentors and invest time and energy in developing their team members. They can identify potential, nurture talent, and help individuals grow professionally, leading to better team performance and succession planning.

7. **They advocate for the team.** These leaders can effectively represent their team's interests at higher organizational levels. They can negotiate for resources, defend their team's work, and ensure their efforts are recognized.

The power and influence of an influential leader extend far beyond their accomplishments. They are catalysts for the growth, success, and well-being of their teams and organizations, and their influence can even impact their industry and the community at large.

HOW INFLUENCE IMPROVES LEADERSHIP SKILLS

Influence is a powerful tool that can significantly improve your leadership skills. Here's how.

1. **Build trust.** When you're an influential leader, people are more likely to trust you. You've proven through your actions and integrity that you're dependable. This trust fosters loyalty and makes it easier for you to lead and motivate your team.

2. **Greater persuasiveness.** Influence allows you to persuade others more effectively. Whether it's selling your vision to the team, pushing through new strategies, or

negotiating with external partners, having influence strengthens your power of persuasion.

3. **Effective conflict resolution.** Influence can help resolve conflict. When you are perceived as a fair and respected person, your team members are more likely to accept your mediation and leadership in conflicts, leading to faster and more harmonious resolutions.

4. **Drive change.** As an influential leader, it becomes easier to drive change. Employees are more willing to follow your lead and adapt to new initiatives or strategies, which reduces resistance and speeds up implementation.

5. **Attract talent.** Influential leaders typically attract talented employees who want to work under their leadership. This can lead to stronger teams and better organizational performance.

6. **Mentoring.** Your influence can improve your ability to mentor and develop others. Your employees will be more willing to seek and value your advice, leading to better individual performance and growth.

7. **Greater autonomy.** When you have some influence, higher-level managers or board members often give you more autonomy. This allows you to do your job better and make decisions more effectively.

8. **Influence beyond the organization.** Your influence as a leader can extend beyond your organization and allow you to shape industry trends, influence community developments, and significantly impact society.

Using your influence responsibly can help you improve your leadership skills, ultimately leading to a more motivated, cohesive team and a more successful company.

HOW IMPORTANT IT IS TO BE A LEADER TO LOOK UP TO

Being a leader that others look up to is important for many reasons. It's not just about being admired, but it contributes greatly to your leadership's effectiveness and your business's success. Here are the reasons why:

1. **Inspiration and motivation.** Admired leaders inspire and motivate their teams. When team members see a leader who is passionate, committed, and fair, they are more likely to aspire to those traits, which improves their performance and engagement.

2. **Trust and loyalty.** When people look up to you as a leader, they trust you. Trust is essential to any successful relationship, especially within a team. When employees trust their leader, they are more likely to be loyal to the company, resulting in lower turnover and higher productivity.

3. **Effective communication.** Admired leaders communicate openly with their teams. Employees feel comfortable sharing their ideas, concerns, and desires, leading to invaluable insights and fostering transparency and collaboration.

4. **Better collaboration.** When team members respect and look up to their leader, they are more likely to collaborate and work toward common goals. This can lead to better team cohesion, less conflict, and better overall performance.

5. **Lead by example.** Leaders who are looked up to serve as role models. Their actions and behavior set the standard for expected behavior within the organization. They have the power to shape the corporate culture and ethical standards.

6. **Greater influence.** A leader you look up to has more influence. Your team is more likely to follow you, embrace change, and buy into your vision, which increases your effectiveness as a leader.

7. **Leadership development.** When you are an admired leader, you also produce new leaders. Those who look up to you will likely emulate your leadership style, creating a pipeline of strong leaders within the organization.

Being a leader others can look up to is not about ego or status; it's about inspiring others, gaining trust, and setting the right example. This requires humility, integrity, and a genuine interest in the well-being of your team. Ultimately, such leadership can significantly increase the success and sustainability of your business.

AWAKEN PRIDE IN YOUR TEAM

An essential aspect of influential leadership is to inspire a sense of pride in your team. Pride leads to better team morale, greater engagement, higher productivity, and stronger loyalty. Here are some strategies to inspire pride in your team.

1. **Celebrate successes.** Recognize and celebrate your team's successes. Recognizing these accomplishments boosts morale and provides a sense of accomplishment, whether they are big wins or small successes. Recognition can take many forms, from a simple thank you to official awards or public commendations.

2. **Create a shared vision.** A shared vision can bind a team and give them a sense of purpose. Involve your team in setting this vision and ensure everyone feels connected to it and understands their role in achieving

it. When team members see their work's impact on the common goal, it inspires a sense of pride.

3. **Foster a positive culture.** Ensure an inclusive, respectful, and supportive team culture. Encourage collaboration and open communication. A positive work environment where everyone feels valued can significantly increase team pride.

4. **Provide growth opportunities.** Provide opportunities for learning and advancement. Encourage team members to improve their skills, take on new challenges, and grow professionally. The pride that comes from personal growth and success can turn into fulfillment in the team and the company.

5. **Lead by example.** Be a leader your team can admire. Model the values and behaviors you want your team to emulate. Your commitment, integrity, and passion can inspire pride in your team.

6. **Empower your team.** Give your team the autonomy and resources they need to do their jobs effectively. Trusting your team to make decisions and solve problems builds confidence and fosters a sense of ownership and pride in their work.

7. **Foster team identity.** Encourage a strong sense of team identity. This can be done through team-building activities, creating team traditions, or even something as simple as clothing or accessories with the team logo. When people feel they belong to a unique group, it creates a sense of belonging and pride.

Your team's pride doesn't happen overnight. It takes consistent effort and genuine care for your team members. But the investment is worth it and results in an engaged, motivated, and productive team.

THE IMPORTANCE OF TRUST IN LEADERSHIP

Trust is a fundamental cornerstone of effective leadership. It is critical in the functioning, cohesion, and success of teams and organizations. Here's why trust in leadership is so important.

1. **Improved communication.** when team members trust their leader, open and honest communication is encouraged. Individuals feel more comfortable expressing their ideas, concerns, and feedback, which leads to better decision-making and problem-solving.

2. **Better collaboration.** Trust fosters a collaborative environment. Team members are more likely to collaborate, share information, and support each other when they trust their leader.

3. **Improved engagement.** When employees have confidence in their leader's decisions and actions, they are more likely to be engaged and invested in their work. They are more motivated to contribute to the organization's goals, which leads to higher productivity.

4. **Empowerment.** Confidence enables leaders to delegate tasks effectively. They can delegate responsibility to their team and empower them to take ownership of their work, boosting morale and job satisfaction.

5. **More innovation.** Trust creates a safe environment where team members feel comfortable taking risks. This is important for innovation because it allows for experimentation, learning from mistakes, and ultimately breakthroughs.

6. **Less resistance to change.** Change, small or large, is part of the life of any organization. When the team trusts its leader, it is more likely to embrace change and quickly adapt because it knows the leader is steering it in the right direction.

7. **Attract and retain talent.** High levels of trust can help attract and retain top talent. When employees trust their leaders, they are more likely to stay with the company, which reduces turnover and associated costs.

8. **Leadership development.** Leaders who have built trust are more likely to develop new leaders. Trust builds the foundation for mentoring relationships and makes it easier to accept feedback and advice.

Building trust doesn't happen overnight; it requires consistent effort, transparency, integrity, and demonstration of competence over time. But once built, trust can become one of a leader's most valuable assets and foster a thriving and productive work environment.

The "leading by influence" paradigm provides a compelling framework for leadership that transforms individual leaders and the organizations they lead. This model goes beyond the conventional realm of leadership and merges with the concept of a visionary CEO — a person who has a clear purpose, can foresee the future, and can inspire others.

Leaders must articulate a unique, transformative message on this journey from obscurity to influence. This transition requires self-reflection, understanding, and a commitment to the why behind the pursuit of influence.

To become an influential leader — or a visionary CEO — you must expand your reach and refine the content of your influence. It's about embodying leadership that others admire, creating a sense of pride within the team, and creating an environment of trust.

Trust is a key element of this leadership model. It promotes open communication, encourages collaboration, and increases engagement. It empowers team members, drives innovation, and enables effective change management. Trust in leadership is the foundation for attracting and retaining talent, developing future leaders, and ensuring the continuity of the company's vision.

An influential leader or visionary CEO recognizes that influence goes beyond the individual. It impacts team dynamics, permeates corporate culture, and contributes to the company's overall success. It opens the door to continuous learning and growth and allows leaders to make a lasting impact.

Ultimately, "leading through influence" is not a destination but a journey. It is a journey marked by mindfulness, commitment, and a passion to effect change. Along the way, leaders will discover their potential, unlock the untapped potential of their teams, and create a legacy that will reverberate throughout their organizations for years to come.

ABOUT THE AUTHOR

I make leaders influential by turning them into an international bestselling author and featuring them on the cover of Pivot, a leading business magazine that reaches over 30 million people.

I discovered the fastest way to help other people change, create real authority, and transform lives, was through books. When you write a book or even a magazine article, people look at you differently. You're the expert. They look up to you. And more importantly—they listen.

Over the past 16 years, my team and I at JETLAUNCH Publishing have designed and published over 14,000 books for clients such as Joe Vitale, John Lee Dumas, and Rachel Pedersen. Providing a seamless experience for authors, we focus on their strengths and message while taking care of all the technical aspects.

As a publishing expert, I've helped executive-level authors build their brands, grow their authority, and attract their ideal clients. By leveraging the power of publishing, I maximize the success of every author I work with, providing them with a platform to share their expertise and make a difference.

As an owner and managing partner of the Strategic Advisor Board, I've had the opportunity to contribute to the success of high-profile clients, including CEOs, multi-millionaires, and even Super Bowl champions. This experience has allowed me to sharpen my skills in strategy, negotiation, and collaboration, further enhancing my ability to support my clients.

One project I'm particularly proud of is *Pivot Magazine*, where we feature interviews with high-level leaders such as General David Petraeus (former director of the CIA), Robert Kiyosaki (Rich Dad, Poor Dad), and Leigh Steinberg (the real Jerry Maguire). These thought-provoking conversations offer readers valuable insights into leadership, innovation, and success.

If you're ready to be a bestselling author, amplify your message, and make a meaningful impact, let's connect!

Send me an email at chris@jetlaunch.net to transform your ideas into a legacy.

Balancing Business Innovation and Risk-Taking with Stability

Jon Hoerauf

The modern business climate is one of ongoing change and renewal. While foundational business principles such as honesty and commitment remain consistent, the structures we build on those foundations continue to change. For instance, there were decades, even in our modern age, when keeping track of sales from the register tape was an adequate method of accounting. The thought of online sales or the use of payment apps was not even considered by most.

However, the speed of technological growth has increased exponentially since the introduction of the home computer and later the offering of the internet to every household. I knew the owner of a small bookstore who relied on sending out a sales catalog twice a year to bring in extra sales. For several years this method worked very well for him.

However, he didn't anticipate that his competition would transfer from the other bookstores within driving distance to larger online discount outlets. He began to see that some of these online stores offered lower book prices than he could compete with and even lower than he could buy himself. I encouraged him to at least offer his goods online, but he didn't think he could maintain this, so he decided instead to change the look and feel of his local store to compete.

Now, after thirty years of business, his empty building stands as a testament to the lack of vision. No one can see the future, and very few could have foreseen the technological explosion we have experienced. But we can all take the time to check the pulse of the world around us to know when it is time to change. Visionary CEOs don't see the future and may not personally have the skill set to face it when it comes, but they are open to change.

They see their business as a living and growing organism that needs to be nourished and maintained rather than controlled. Visionary CEOs don't hold on to traditions but also don't change just because it's popular. They don't gamble the lives of their businesses on the latest leadership book or market trends. They know themselves and their values.

They have a strong and lasting purpose statement by which they live. They know that while the soul of their dream doesn't change, the method of carrying out that dream may change several times over their business life. Visionary CEOs have their fingers on the pulse of their business and its needs for today while scanning the horizon to see what adjustments need to be made to weather any upcoming storms.

One summer, I had the opportunity to help a local farmer plow his fields. I quickly learned that if you want to plow straight rows, you can't spend your energy looking down at the field, looking back to see how you are doing, or even focusing your attention several yards ahead of the tractor. To make straight rows, you need to choose a fixed object at the far end of the field and focus on that while driving the tractor.

A Visionary CEO can balance a willingness to alter the course of their practices based on upcoming changes in the environment with the grit to stay true to their mission at all costs.

I was in college when the first PCs hit the market. In school, we had access to a mainframe computer that displayed on monitors with green letters on a black background. One semester, I had a sixty-page paper that I needed to print, so I sent it to the dot matrix printer and went to bed because it printed so slowly.

When it was time to consider buying something for myself, I went to the local Radio Shack and asked the salesman to convince me that I should get a PC rather than a typewriter. In my mind, he couldn't convince me that it was worth it, which was short-sighted on my part.

A couple of years later, I was working on an internship, and the internet came on the scene. My supervisor was very excited about it and showed me how to check the weather in any location worldwide. I was not impressed and passed on this new technology—again, very short-sighted.

As I watched the dotcoms come and go and merge into online buying, I realized that I had completely missed what was right in front of me because I was unwilling to see the potential of something I didn't understand. Years later, I worked as an instructional designer in the e-learning department at a college. I found myself frustrated with the college leadership as I tried to convince them that the way to grow is to invest in online learning rather than focus merely on face-to-face instruction.

While the members of an organization look to the CEO for the vision, it's important for them to feel like they have a voice in it. If employees feel like the vision is getting done *to* them, they can easily see their job as an assembly line production that they only participate in for the check. This doesn't mean that every employee needs to have a say in what the vision for the organization is, but they need to feel like they have an effective role in carrying out that vision and a voice in its future evolution.

If a solid vision is already in place, then it is the job of the CEO to instill that vision in the hearts of the rest of the team. They need to feel the same passion the CEO felt when the vision was first created. The vision is the energy that compels the organization forward; without it, the whole thing can quickly come to a halt.

If a CEO is still creating their vision, involving key team members from across the organization in its development would be helpful. Ultimately, the CEO is responsible for the final draft, but input from the whole team (or representatives from the various teams) will not only help assure long-term buy-in but will also open more doors for creativity.

There is often a blur between the definitions of mission and vision. For this example, I consider the mission of an organization or team as a statement of their purpose, whom they will help, what they will accomplish, etc. The vision is a statement of how they will achieve this.

A CEO can create a comprehensive vision of their path forward by looking at the most effective practices already employed within the organization, researching what others find helpful, and drawing from the creative brainpower of the existing team. Ultimately, all of this information must be distilled into an understandable statement or infographic so everyone on the team can easily understand and explain the vision to others.

Balancing innovation/risk-taking and maintaining organizational stability is vital and challenging. First, a CEO needs to do a bit of self-reflection. They need to take some time away to honestly appraise where they are personally on the spectrum between risk-taking and maintaining stability. It's impossible to create balance before one is aware of their natural preference on this scale.

There is a need for both innovation/risk-taking and stable, sustainable growth. This means that no matter where someone is now, they need to be willing to move into an uncomfortable or even fearful zone if they want to create this balance. Ultimately, some businesses will lean toward risk-taking, and others will lean toward stability, but no matter the business, there is always a balance to maintain.

Once leaders discover their own preferences and apprehensions, they can develop a plan for walking out this balance. This might involve a trusted team member who leans toward the opposite direction, finding a mentor, or intentionally pushing themselves into new areas. Whichever avenue they choose, it will be helpful to adopt a mindset that experimentation, not perfection, is a mark of success.

There is no end to great ideas and emails suggesting ways your company can save money, improve efficiency, or reach more people. A clear vision allows you to quickly sift through the myriad ideas and offers and pick the one or two worth exploring. I'm presently rebuilding a department that has recently come under my supervision. Somehow, the entire internet seems to know of this new position and is emailing me great programs that will change my life.

Many of these sound interesting, but there is no time to explore each one. I'm evaluating the long-term vision of this department, which out of necessity, will be much different than it has been in the past. Part of this evaluation is looking at the technology presently used to determine if it will meet our future needs or must be replaced.

In this process, I need to consider both the cost of replacement and retraining if we choose a new program. Once this decision is made, I can determine what technology will best meet the needs of my new vision for this department, and only then will I begin to explore options to meet those needs.

The most important thing a CEO can do to foster a growth mindset is deal with their pride. We want to think that we have arrived and are the go-to in our field. We all can grow, and the only way to grow is to be open to the fact that most other people in the world can teach us something.

A growth mindset embraces trial and error and believes that high-level skills come with practice. We are not born superstars. You have room to grow even if you are naturally prone to excel in something. If you refuse to grow, someone else who is not afraid of trying, failing, and trying again will eventually surpass you. The more we embrace failure as our friend and mentor, the further we will get in our pursuits.

The most effective way for me to manage stress is through my spiritual connection. Knowing that someone bigger than me is interested in my well-being brings comfort when I feel overwhelmed and peace when the bottom falls out. Also, I spend as much time in nature as I can.

I love to garden because it allows me to nurture plants throughout their life span and enjoy the tangible results of my efforts. I love walking barefoot in the grass and going for long bike rides with my wife. These bring me joy and fulfillment beyond what work accomplishments can provide.

I believe fostering a sense of curiosity with my team is vital. Asking questions and trying to solve unsolvable problems encourages innovation personally and professionally. Getting stuck in a system of doing things the way they have always been done leads to a slow and painful death to our souls. Asking your team to help with the problem-solving process keeps them fresh and sharp and opens up an avenue of resources that the CEO wouldn't have otherwise.

Many avenues can be used to elicit their input. It can be as simple as a group email asking for ideas, a focus group assembled for a specific problem, or even a competition to see who comes up with the best idea for change. I took over a department suffering from discontent and infighting between the more experienced and newer team members.

At one point, one of the old guard approached me to complain that one of the newbies had messed up a shared document. When I checked with the accused member, I found out she did not delete the information. I solved the issue by putting the two of them on a team to revamp the process to prevent data from accidentally getting deleted. The result was a new and improved process. More importantly, the two employees developed respect and trust for each other, and I did not have to spend time developing the new process.

I have developed several habits to maintain and strengthen my CEO mindset. I get up early every morning to ensure I have time to myself before my day begins. Some days I read, some days I journal, and some days I walk around my backyard with a cup of coffee, enjoying the sunrise. Starting my day this way helps me refresh before heading to the office. I also read regularly from a growing library of books on leadership, change, and empowerment.

New leaders need to give themselves time to learn and grow. The best way to learn how to lead others is to seek out leadership roles either as a volunteer, on a sports team, or within your present circle of influence at work. Leading doesn't mean bossing people around, and it's not limited to those over whom you have some power. You can lead your supervisor or your teammates with a positive, servant attitude and effect change from the side or back of the group.

Good leaders need to know themselves and their style of leading. Don't try to copy someone else; find yourself and develop your strong points. Finally, practice humility, admit your mistakes, and always be open to learning, even from the most unlikely people.

SUMMARY

- The modern business climate requires constant change and adaptation, driven primarily by technological advances. He emphasizes the need for companies to adapt to these changes to remain competitive.

- The author emphasizes the role of visionary CEOs who are open to change and see their company as an evolving entity. They must stay true to their mission while responding to environmental changes.

- The author shares personal experiences of missing opportunities by resisting new technologies. Later, they argue for the importance of online learning in education and emphasize the need to adapt and innovate.

- The author emphasizes the importance of employee engagement in achieving a company's vision. Employees should feel they have a role in achieving the vision and have a say in the company's future development.

- The balance between innovation and risk-taking and maintaining stability is discussed. The author suggests that CEOs should consider their position on this spectrum and find ways to achieve balance, such as involving trusted team members or mentors.

- The author talks about the importance of having a clear vision to sift through the many ideas and identify the most promising ones. Restructuring a department is given as an example.

- The importance of fostering a growth mindset is emphasized. CEOs should be open to new ideas, engage in trial and error, and view high competency as something that is learned over time.

- The author presents personal stress management strategies, such as cultivating a spiritual connection and spending time in nature.

- He advocates fostering curiosity within the team. This can be achieved by encouraging problem-solving and involving team members in decision-making processes.

- The author provides personal routines and advice for aspiring leaders, such as taking time to learn, seeking leadership opportunities, and practicing humility.

ACTION STEPS

1. **Rethink your position:** After reading the author's insights, take some time to think about yourself and figure out where you personally stand on the spectrum between risk-taking and stability. Understanding your own preferences is the first step to a balanced approach in your business.

2. **Involve your team:** Use the author's examples to find ways to foster curiosity in your team. This may mean encouraging them to solve complex problems or asking them to participate in new initiatives. Such participation can lead to innovative solutions and an engaged and productive workforce.

3. **Develop a growth mindset:** Take inspiration from the author's discussion on fostering a growth mindset. Be open to failure as a learning opportunity, enjoy experimentation, and remember that high skills come with

practice. Incorporating this mindset into your culture will help you continuously improve and succeed in the long run.

ABOUT THE AUTHOR

Jon Hoerauf has a background as a counselor and teacher. He is a writer and professional speaker in the areas of motivation, leadership, and teamwork. To schedule him for a workshop or as a keynote speaker, you can contact him at jon@JonHoerauf.com.

The Importance of a Visionary CEO in a Rapidly Changing World

Leslee Moss Cohen

What key characteristics distinguish a visionary CEO from a traditional one, and why are they essential in today's business world?

A visionary CEO must be driven by endless curiosity. She is always learning and incentivizes her team to do the same. As has been repeatedly said, the only certainty is change. Every industry is in a constant state of flux and if you are only focused on the tasks immediately in front of you, the world will pass you by and your business will slowly fail. In today's environment, a main focus should be on keeping up with new technologies that will increase efficiency, thereby affecting your bottom line. If you instead remain stagnant, your clients will inevitably become aware of your being behind the times and uncertain as to whether they are getting the best products and services for their investment in your business. This also applies to potential employees, who want to trust that their chosen organization will stand the test of time.

To gain this ever evolving expertise, a visionary CEO must participate in networking and mastermind groups. She must also read, listen to and attend applicable and educational publications, podcasts and programs in an effort to learn both the hot topics that her competitors are grappling with and to gain insights regarding what other industries are facing that might become relevant to her own business down the road.

The business I operate is a boutique corporate law firm and lawyers as a whole are known to be particulary risk-averse. They are also generally behind the curve regarding technology, social media andother new business trends. For this reason, I have chosen to become involved with outside organizations that give me access to other lawyers, but equally important, the owners of other types of businesses. Perhaps my most meaningful time not in the office is spent on the Executive Committee and Board of Directors of the Small Business Advocacy Council of Illinois. The SBAC is a non-partisan organization focused on advocating for small businesses at the local, state and national levels. First of all, the work done by the SBAC is beneficial for my clients, almost all of which are small businesses. Secondly, my colleagues in the organization consist of several lawyers but also people who operate entities offering an endless variety of products and services. The exposure to all of them is invaluable to the ability of my own firm to innovate and improve.

I will share a few examples of how my business has benefitted from my zest for acquiring new knowledge. One is the model that my firm has developed in terms of who we employee. We hire people nationwide who need to work part-time for different reasons. Some are caring for young children, others for elderly parents. Some worked 50+ hour weeks at large law firms for several years and want to spend more time travelling. I developed this model during the course of a services business accelerator program called "Powerful Partners" that

I participated in after my long-time partner retired. He had been running the firm while I was raising my two boys, developing a client base and practicing law.

When I took over operations, we experienced rapid growth, and I had absolutely no idea how to run a business. The year long program included full day sessions on financials, marketing, scaling, leadership and so much more. We were also guided through the process of differentiating our businesses in the marketplace in order to attract and retain not only customers but top talent. Adopting this hiring model gave me access to some extraordinarily top notch lawyers who were unable to work full time and/or in person. In my ongoing quest for continued education, I have recently heard about other law firms that have a similar hiring model and have grown to fifty or more lawyers and, in response, immediately reach out to each of their managing partners for insight and guidance. It's a mindset of constant curiosity.

Another example relates to the need to remain abreast of new technologies. Our lawyers are focused on representing early stage companies from seed to exit. As startups grow through the process of equity fundraising, they add investors to their ownership structure and the investments those investors make have varying terms depending on the "round" of capital being raised. In recent years, a "cap table" management tool called Carta has become industry standard for managing complex capitalization structures. Having a law firm partnership with Carta and a deep familiarity with its regular updates is one of the indicators that I find clients rely on for ensuring that our firm is up to date on the technology that is vital for their companies' success. It's also incumbent upon our team to remain current with the ongoing new tools Carta offers that can be helpful to our clients.

A visionary CEO not only has to keep learning, but also must incentivize her employees to stay on top of industry trends. I find that my younger team members are especially in tune with what is new and innovative in the world. Accordingly, the entire firm benefits when those employees feel heard and know they will be met with respect when then come to me with new ideas.

One of the lawyers in my firm approached me recently to note that she was interested in ChatGPT and how our firm might use that tool. There have been ongoing discussion regarding the fear of artificial intelligence replacing corporate lawyers like us who spend most days drafting contracts for clients. This young woman's idea was to figure out how to implement ChatGPT and other AI technologies into our practice so as to improve our efficiency for clients, show that we are staying current with the times and, in the process, hopefully demonstrate the continued necessity of our own services. I pay this particular lawyer on an hourly basis so in response to her interest in learning about ChatGPT, I readily agreed to pay her to research the topic and put together a presntation to educate the other lawyers, although it was non-billable work. Her knowledge would not only be crucial for our client but, perhaps, even more importantly, sent the signal that I supported her ideas about improving our firm.

What pivotal moment or experience in your career as a leader inspired you to adopt a visionary mindset, and how has this mindset influenced your approach to leadership, strategy, and organizational growth?

Participating in the Powerful Partners program to learn how to operate and scale a business was the most pivotal moment in my career as a leader. The other women I met and became remarkably close with inspired me to adopt a visionary mindset. Crucially, none of them were lawyers. A requirement for program enrollment was having achieved career success in the past. On the very first day, we shared the stories of those successes and what had led us to pivot towards the path of starting a new business with the goal of growing and scaling. Then, we were each required to identify a "North Star," basically exactly what we wanted to get out of the program during its one year tenure.

My North Star was pretty bland at first....I wanted to build a sustainable law firm. That seemed like a big enough challenge to me, but when the program leader reached out to hone that North Star, she asked a critical question I had never thought to ask myself, "Where do you, Leslee Cohen, fit into this business, this law firm you want to build?" That was my AH HAH moment: *Wow, I can build something great here that reflects my values, and makes a difference in the world that is unique to who I am.* Hence, the development of my hiring model discussed above.

While law firms usually don't lend themselves to either remote or flexible work arrangements, I was actually one of the first lawyers I knew afforded the opportunity to work part-time all the way back in 1998. During my parenting years, I was able to be the lawyer I wanted to be and the mom I wanted to be--it was rare and it was fantastic and it was an the experience I wanted to pass on.

Powerful Partners also impressed upon me how much time and effort are involved in running a business. The coolest thing is, though, that if you do that—work ON the business instead of only working IN the business—you can effectively grow and scale and build something incredibly fulfilling and successful that reflects who you are.

My partner's retirement coincided with my own new status as an empty nester and little did I realize the extent of the shift and how ready I was for a new chapter. In the past, I had been entirely content practicing law with my partner and one administrative employee. My days were intellectually challenging and busy. However, I became more and more excited as I dug in to the Powerful Partners program, to all the facets of running a business, and then adding my own personal touch and mission. I've always loved learning, and I couldn't wait to tackle this new challenge in addition to practicing law. The firm grew quickly after implementing the basics I learned.

In the spirit of becoming a visionary CEO, after a few years, I decided to find an executive coach. I had lost an amazing team member, and wanted to prevent that from reoccurring. I knew I had to step up as a leader which was still out of my comfort zone to some degree, leading to the decision to engage my coach who primarily works with lawyers and law firms but also with other business owners. She has helped me communicate more effectively and more regularly with my team, implement systems and processes and strategically plan each year for the future. She also runs a group of law firm owners who meet monthly, which has helped me stay aware of other firms and how they are resolving the issues we all face. That way, my firm keeps abreast of its market and is often even ahead of the curve.

I also started down the road of social media marketing. Traditionally, lawyer-client relationships were developed through very personal relationship building. However, I had learned through Powerful Partners, my coach and other networking experiences that many clients now search for their lawyers online, such that an active social media presence seemed to be becoming beneficial if not necessary. I spoke to ten different marketing firms before hiring the one I chose—each of which had a different take on strategy and a different fee structure. I believe that a visionary CEO outsources to specialists but does a huge amount of due diligence iin selecting those specialists. I asked for references from every one I interviewed to ensure that other users had a good experience with them.

How can a CEO develop a compelling vision for their organization, and how does this vision impact overall company strategy?

I started developing my vision by brainstorming to compile a list of everything important to me about the firm I wanted to create and lead.

My very first thought was of the team I wanted to build and to make sure that each team member liked what they were doing, which meant I had to learn each one of their strengths, the areas that they enjoyed practicing in, and their personality types in order to match them with the right clients. I also wanted them to feel appreciated, valued, and part of something bigger than themselves. I connected with a consulting team that specializes in team building and integrated regular team building sessions into our firm's calendar. In one meeting, we identified each others' superpowers and brainstormed about how to use them for the benefit of each other and the firm as a whole. In another, we identified the firm's current state and goals for the future and mapped out how to get there— intertwined with being blindfolded and depending on each other to get through an obstacle course! We kept up these sessions even during COVID. Although we met on Zoom, this together time definitely helped keep us bound as one organization. I also schedule one-on-one calls with each lawyer in the firm every month, in addition to our weekly team call. I think communication constant communication—with your team is very important.

My second focus in developing a compelling vision for the firm was the client experience. Of the highest importance by far was having highly skilled attorneys and offering the utmost expertise in our field. Next was wanting to change the paradigm of big law as acting super professional and serious, and buttoned up. I wanted to create a firm where we educate—not intimidate—our clients. I wanted each client to feel listened to and understood and not scared that the clock would start ticking the second I picked up their call.

I also didn't want the firm to be all about how many hours we could bill. Each of our lawyers comes from a large firm, and I knew from my twenty years in big law that the pressure at those firms is to bill hours. So I have had to change each one of my lawyer's mindsets when they first start at our firm to "how I can be most efficient while still best protecting the client from a legal perspective."

After all of this brainstorming, I integrated all of my thoughts and ideas into a vision statement. However, it's very important to note that vision is not static, and neither is my vision statement. I am constantly updating it as I learn from newsletters, presentations, podcasts, webinars, books, networking groups and masterminds.

Vision is extraordinarily important for overall company strategy because, as you move forward, it is the pedestal on which the entire organization rests. If I find myself unsure how to approach an HR or client issue or whether to make an offer to a potential new employee, for example, I reread that vision statement, which always guides me in the right direction. Additionally, we regularly repeat the vision statement during team meetings, to keep all of us in the mindset of its pillars.

How does a visionary CEO balance innovation and risk-taking with maintaining stability and sustainable growth in the organization?

I will go back to having that vision statement to guide your decision-making in response to this question. It's a matter of creating a platform and building on it. I rarely stop a practice I've developed for the group, the firm, or clients; instead, I add more communication or develop more firm forms.

It's important to listen to your people often rather than talk at them. For instance, I used to feel very uncomfortable during our weekly team meetings. They just didn't seem to flow well. The format back then consisted of each taking a turn describing current projects being undertaken. During one of our team building sessions, I discovered that everyone was just plain bored at those meetings. I asked for feedback from the group and learned that they wanted the chance to raise issues and challenges they were facing individually and get advice from each other. Since we implemented the change, our meetings are much more interactive and enjoyable. That's what a visionary CEO does--communicates with her employees, asking what they think, and making changes to address their feedback in response.

Another way to maintain stability while innovating is to know when to slow down and when to put the pedal to the metal. When my firm added two new lawyers within a one year period, I decided to work on integrating them well with the clients and the firm before focusing on further growth. Each new employee adds time consuming administrative work, and the need to train that employee on "how we do it at AllRise," such as how we interact with clients, how we handle billing, how we communicate with each other and so much more. Growing too fast is not always the best option. In a product based business, you may be able to make more money by scaling faster, but a service based company is not selling widgets. As a law firm, each lawyer's personality, skill set, and how they fit with the clients is critical to how your clients perceive their experience with the firm.

Additionally, as you grow, you will need to implement more systems and processes because you, as the leader, cannot possibly be everything to everyone. After adding those two new lawyers, we added a paralegalto service those lawyers. Then, after adding the paralegal, we switched to an outsourced book-keeper because our COO became too overwhelmed with all of the bookkeeping and dealing with more employees and growing client base that we were servicing as our team increased.

Can you share a personal experience that demonstrates the impact of visionary leadership on an organization's success? What lessons can be learned from this experience?

As I touched on above, part of my vision was not to be a firm centered on billing time. As a law firm leader charged with bringing in clients, I am often asked "what's your billable hourly rate?" In response, I try to explain to clients that our hourly rates are actually less important than the motivation underlying each attorney's work. In big law, the pressure is to bill X number of hours a year, with the repercussions of not meeting those targets being reduced compensation. This is necessarily the model in order to be profitable in the face of tremendous overhead and budgets but it is not the model I wanted for own my firm.

Our lawyers work with predominantly with small businesses, entrepreneurs and startups that don't have the budget for a billing based law firm. However, maintaining financial health as a law firm using efficiency as a parameter is a lot easier said than done—which is where vision plays a major role. One of our practice areas is the review and negotiation of day-to-day contracts. During the course of building the firm, I realized that clients tended to become very upset if we spent too much time reviewing and revising a contract between that client's small business and a much larger company, meaning a lop-sided negotiating power structure between the two parties.

In the spirit of communicating with my team and consistently reminding them of my respect for their advice, I finally raised this issue with one of my team members, and together we came up with what she has branded as the "Goldilocks" approach. We now offer clients three levels of contract review. Level one is recognizing that a contract is between a small business client and a larger company with substantially more negotiating leverage. In these cases, our attorneys only review for the potential pitfalls that could be deal breakers such that our client may want to avoid entering into this contract altogether. Level two is reviewing the contract and commenting on the provisions that are bothersome to us as lawyers. Our client then guides us as to which such provisions matter to them as business owners before we spend the time (and legal dollars) actually revising the contract. Level three review is reserved for contracts pivotal to a client's business. For instance, the form of contract they will proffer to all of their customers. In these circumstances, our lawyers must review the contract in-depth and revise it to the point of perfection.

Each of these three approaches lead to very different amounts of time spent and dollars billed to the client. Offering choices has made a tremendous difference because our clients appreciate that we care enough to delve into their individual needs and that we are making the effort to keep their bills in check as opposed to the reputation most lawyers have for basking in the delight of starting the hourly billing clock.

Along the same lines, we have also developed many firm forms that create major efficiencies, and offer to provide those forms to our clients and let them take a first shot at filling them in for our editing, again saving legal costs. I also have become a huge fan of term sheets bullet pointing out all of the major issues involved in a transaction, contract, or agreement before drafting these long documents. This way, if the two sides are not yet in agreement on terms, we avoid the time consuming process of revising whole versions. Similarly, I favor detailed letters of intent in connection with mergers and acquisitions and investor term sheets.

We have also developed questionnaires for shareholder agreements, limited liability company agreements and employment agreements so clients can complete them and come to an agreement on terms before we spend the time preparing lengthy documents. We think a great deal about saving money for our clients as opposed to the large law firm model, and we find them to be extremely appreciative of those efforts.

How can a CEO cultivate a growth mindset and foster a culture of continuous learning and improvement within their organization?

A visionary CEO lets her team know she values their opinions and input. I have learned over a thirty-year plus career that as much as I have very strong opinions, the sum is much greater when you combine each of the separate parts. In making hiring choices, I'm always thinking about whether a candidate is someone whose advice I will value in my own decision making process. There's definitely an ongoing balancing act between acting as a leader, on the one hand, and expressing openness to your employees' input and then acting on that input so they know you were really listening and that their opinions truly meant something to you.

To foster that mindset of improving the firm as a whole, I go back to the concept of constant communication. Having one-on-one calls, at least monthly, to ask team members: How can we improve the firm? How has your month been? What's one thing that's not working for you or one improvement you can think of to make to the organization? Ask your employees to make presentations on an area of expertise for the whole team regularly so they can learn from each other and to remind them your goal is not a top-down structure but instead everyone working together and learning to value each other's input.

Encourage your team to feel comfortable bringing issues to the whole group for input and not just to the leader. Be humble enough to tell your people in words and in deeds "I don't know everything. I need your help, and I need that diversity of thought. I need to know what you're thinking." You may not necessarily choose to implement every single suggestion, and in those cases be certain to communicate your appreciation for the thoughts together with an explanation that your ultimate decision was made taking into account the best interest of the entire organization rather than any one individual. As long as they know that you value them, and that when you go in a different direction, it's because you are thinking of the whole firm, they will trust that you are making the right decision.

One other tip…. never play favorites within the firm and do not discuss any team member with the others. This is sometimes difficult but if you are bad mouthing one employee to another, she will wonder what you are saying to others about her. This cycle is deadly to the culture of your organization, cultivating competition and mistrust.. You can talk to your executive coach, a personal board of advisors that many CEOs put together and lean on or trusted friends and family members. Keeping cattiness out of the organization is vital.

How do you manage stress and maintain mental well-being as an entrepreneur, and what self-care practices have been most effective for you?

I do many different things to manage stress and maintain mental well-being. First, having an executive coach has been extraordinarily helpful to me. Having someone on your side who is there to listen and run ideas past and someone strong enough to say, "I don't think that's the way to handle it," has been crucial to the success of the firm.

Next, exercise is non-negotiable. I take group exercise classes, so the times I'm in those classes are blocked on my calendar. Period. Clients do not need to know whether I'm dealing with a medical issue with my parents or whether I'm at a workout class or whatever else I am engaged in. I tell them when I am available rather than when I'm not.

I also spend many many hours networking. When I first started the business, that networking was interspersed within each day which was untenable because I felt whiplashed in different directions all day long. My coach encouraged me to move, again, to the time blocking concept. I've now expanded on that concept to preserve my sanity. Mondays and Thursdays are spent in the office, head down working. On the other days, I set aside time for lunch, team calls and networking. I also created a Calendly account (truly life changing) where I set up two different kinds of meetings. One for networking and one for other calls. Instead of going through that whole process—Are you available this day? Are you available that day? What time?—I simply share my calendar link. If that means I am booked two months in advance, then I am booked two months in advance.

I also think it's very important to stay social. I'm an extroverted introvert, so I don't need to constantly attend huge parties and events. But I think ensuring that you are not isolated, always sitting in front of the computer, is critical. Even in the realm of being social, there's keeping up with friends, but it's also really satisfying to stay social by networking with people you like. The many different kinds of people I've met through networking for professional purposes have vastly expanded my world. We tend to make friends with people with whom we have much in common so this is an opportunity to enrich your life by meeting others outside of that circle.

I was invited to lunch recently with someone I met through business, and we've enjoyed a great referral relationship. Her intention with this lunch was to ask a few of the women whom she has met through networking and believed would benefit from knowing each other. After a delicious and really enjoyable lunch, I not only I made new friends and had social time outside of the office, but I simultaneously started new relationships that ultimately benefitted my business.

I also recommend taking regular vacations. When you run a business, taking vacations requires well thought-out processes and procedures so that the business continues to run smoothly when the owner is unavailable for an extended period of time. I recently took a much longer vacation than ever in my career to Japan. Before leaving I frantically bemoaned to my coach that I would never do this again. Her response was "No, you *will* do it again. We'll build processes and procedures so everything runs smoothly while you're away. When you return we will review what worked and what needs improvement next time." Guess what? It all went pretty well and I'm excited for another long break!

What habits or daily routines have you implemented to help maintain and strengthen your CEO mindset?

One of my closest friends coined a practice that is essential to me: "Respect the lull." This means that when there is downtime for you within the business, when things are slow, instead of panicking that the business will not continue to grow and this is the new normal, enjoy the little bit of freedom you are so rarely afforded. Perhaps step up the networking to console yourself that you are moving the business forward. However, also take advantage of the extra time and know that things will pick up again.

Along the same lines, learn to say no to opportunities you feel most likely will not benefit your business. An example for me are large networking events where I am just part of a huge crowd. If I have received an invitation from a client or a close friend to one of these events and it's important to them that I be there, that's one thing. On the other hand, if it just consists of sitting at a table to celebrate the event of the year of some industry organization that will not directly benefit the firm, I would rather take the time to be with my family or friends.

In terms of my habits and routines, one is meeting with my coach at least monthly. She bills monthly, but there's no cancellation for a year. When I first started working with her, I was afraid of using too much of her time, but she reached out to me and said, "You're paying for my time; you should be using it." Regular meetings with my coach are essential.

Additionally, I prioritize time with my Powerful Partner's group friends on a regular basis. They are my "business besties." During the program we learned so much about each other and it helps to reconnect with people who know my business, me, my team, and the issues I've faced and conquered in the past. You can always put together your own similar group. Identify the people whose advice you value and form a personal board of directors with regularly scheduled meetings.

Listening to podcasts has made a big difference for me as well. When I'm in the car, I trade off listening to music, which I love, for podcasts on long drives. The topics of interest to me are entrepreneurship, business development, and changes within the areas of law that I practice. These podcasts make me feel less lonely as an entrepreneur. They have also strengthened my visionary mindset because I'm constantly reminded of how much I don't know and how many opportunities there are to improve my business.

I also belong to several online platforms. I recently joined The Entreprenista League and another group called Be The Upside. These platforms create a sense of community among their members. Members are regularly crowdsourcing questions like the one I recently raised, "I have a startup client that is building a board of directors, and wants to issue equity grants to thank the directors for being part of this board and incentivize them to continue participating. How much equity is market these days?" One of the platforms focuses on business owners, and another is comprised of highly vetted independent consultants. Again, through these groups I have formed new relationships and learned so much by reading the questions raised throughout each day, as well as the answers, all of which fosters the continued development of my firm.

Mastermind groups are also important. These are groups of people who get to know your business and you and allow you to share insights. Again, hearing the issues that other business owners are facing and the advice they're given is incredibly beneficial because many of those same questions and advice will probably apply to your business too.

What advice would you give to aspiring leaders looking to develop their own visionary mindset and strategic thinking capabilities?

The advice that has helped me grow and flourish is as follows.

First and foremost, find a group of individuals to hold you accountable. Meet with them regularly to share ways to improve your business or solve issues you're grappling with. Ensure that they will ask you during your next meeting whether you took the steps you promised and followed through. Being held accountable will keep you moving forward. The more input you get from all different people, the better. I recently had an issue with one of my team members and thought I knew how to handle it, but before going the very direct route, which is my personality, I ran it by a group of peers. They helped me reframe the way I was going to tackle the issue, and to present it with a "positivity sandwich" starting with *you're so great due to xyz,* then moving to *here's an issue to work on,* and finishing with *you're so great!* In the end, I handled the situation so much better than I had anticipated because I had input from several trusted advisors.

Next, set a North Star. What do you want your business to be? Maybe you do it annually. What do you want to accomplish this year? Then, break that down into specific goals and a timeline to achieve them. Make it realistic with quarterly or monthly goals. Ensure these goals are not seem insurmountable. Break them down into tasks, and break those tasks into specific time frames so you can achieve them.

A few other random tips....create a vision statement, and stay focused. Stay open to always learning more. Consider calls with your competitors--there is enough business to go around. Don't get caught up in the business. Set aside plenty of time to work on the business. Some weeks, you'll have to push it off to the next week, but at least try because you need to accept that improving your business will never end. Your to-do list will never be finished, but keep a running list and try to tackle some of it gradually.

When I say you should work ON the business rather than IN the business, I mean things like networking and developing new customers, stepping back to think about what different kinds of marketing can be implemented, developing a list of all your past speaking engagements and a speaker sheet to describe speeches you are available to deliver. What new forms should you be coming up with? What groups are out there may be beneficial that you haven't joined yet? Always brainstorm how to improve your business rather than getting stuck performing the tasks of the people working within the business. Act as the leader and business owner and business owner you are.

ABOUT THE AUTHOR

Leslee Cohen is the founder and managing partner of AllRise Legal Counsel. AllRise concentrates its transactional practice on securities and startup law, corporate finance, technology law, mergers and acquisitions, and general corporate law. It represents clients across many industries, from consumer products to technology companies to healthcare businesses to real estate firms.

Leslee started her practice at a Wall Street firm in 1992, spent thirteen years honing her skills at a large firm based in Chicago, and left to form AllRise in 2010. AllRise was founded on Leslee's desire to work with earlier-stage and smaller businesses. Each of its attorneys is big-firm trained and experienced.

Leslee has been named by *Illinois Super Lawyers* as one of the Top 100 Lawyers in the State of Illinois and Top 50 Women Lawyers in the State of Illinois, corporate finance and securities, every year since 2010, a *Leading Lawyer in* mergers and acquisitions, securities, and venture finance every year since 2007, the Advocate of the Year by the Small Business Advocacy Council in 2019 and, most recently, an Enterprising Woman of the Year by *Enterprising Women Magazine* and a Top Woman in Law by *Law Bulletin Media*, each in 2023.

She is a member of the Executive Committee and Board of Directors of the Small Business Advocacy Council, the co-chair of the Advisory Committee of the Coalition of Women's Initiatives in Law (of which she is also a co-founder), a speaker and mentor for the Good Food Accelerator, the Hatchery, LegalPad, the Wisconsin Technology Council/the Founders Institute and Workbox, and involved with the Chicago Job Creators Grant organization and GirlCon, which supports high school girls interested in careers in technology.

Leslee received her B.A. from the University of Michigan and her J.D. from New York University School of Law.

Learn more about Leslee at www.allriselawyers.com.

The Visionary CEO: Mastering Mindset, Vision, and Strategy

Joel Phillips

In my years as CEO of Proshark and CTO of the Strategic Advisor Board, I've had the privilege of working closely with a range of leaders, each with their unique styles and approaches. This experience has allowed me to discern some of the key characteristics that distinguish a visionary CEO from a traditional one.

Today's business world is marked by relentless change, uncertainty, and disruption. In such an environment, the role of a CEO requires more than just managing day-to-day operations. It demands foresight, agility, and a mindset that transcends conventional wisdom. Allow me to elaborate on some of these defining traits.

1. **Embracing Innovation Over Tradition**

   Visionary CEO: Constantly seeks new ways to innovate, improve and break the molds of tradition. They are less concerned with how things have been done in the past and more focused on where the business needs to go.

Traditional CEO: Focuses on maintaining the status quo, often relying on time-tested methods and practices.

Why It's Essential: In a rapidly changing world, clinging to traditional methods can lead to stagnation. Embracing innovation allows companies to stay ahead of the curve and adapt to the ever-changing landscape.

2. **Strategic Thinking vs. Tactical Execution**

   Visionary CEO: Engages in long-term strategic thinking, looking beyond the immediate future, and planning for growth and sustainability. They align their decisions with broader goals and a company's mission.

   Traditional CEO: Emphasizes short-term goals and tactical execution, often reacting to immediate pressures without considering long-term implications.

   Why It's Essential: A visionary perspective ensures that a company is prepared for future challenges and opportunities, aligning with larger industry trends and societal needs.

3. **Adaptive Leadership vs. Hierarchical Management**

   Visionary CEO: Practices adaptive leadership by empowering team members, fostering collaboration, and promoting a culture of continuous learning.

   Traditional CEO: Relies on a hierarchical management structure, focusing on control and strict adherence to policies.

   Why It's Essential: Adaptive leadership creates a resilient organization that can adjust to change and foster creativity and innovation.

4. **Emphasis on Purpose and Values**

Visionary CEO: Articulates a clear sense of purpose and aligns the company's values with its actions, inspiring employees and creating a sense of shared mission.

Traditional CEO: Focuses primarily on financial performance and may overlook the importance of organizational culture and values.

Why It's Essential: A strong connection between purpose and values can enhance employee engagement, customer loyalty, and foster a positive brand image.

5. **Willingness to Take Risks**

Visionary CEO: Not afraid to take calculated risks and make bold decisions in the pursuit of groundbreaking achievements.

Traditional CEO: Tends to avoid risk and adheres strictly to established norms.

Why It's Essential: Taking calculated risks can lead to innovation and growth, positioning a company as a leader rather than a follower.

In conclusion, the distinction between a visionary and traditional CEO goes beyond mere management style; it reflects a profound difference in how they perceive and engage with the world. While traditional leadership has its place, the complexities of today's business environment require a visionary approach that emphasizes innovation, strategic thinking, adaptability, value alignment, and a willingness to take risks.

These traits are not just theoretical ideals but essential prerequisites for success in our ever-evolving world. Leaders who cultivate these attributes are more likely to drive their organizations forward, harnessing the opportunities and navigating the challenges that lie ahead. They are the ones who are best equipped to lead in a world that no longer rewards playing it safe but demands bold vision and fearless execution.

The trajectory of a leader's career is often marked by specific moments or experiences that serve as turning points. In my case, the pivotal moment that inspired me to adopt a visionary mindset came early in my tenure as CEO of Proshark.

I recall a particular period when the company was facing unprecedented challenges. We were caught in a highly competitive market, struggling with outdated technology and a business model that was increasingly irrelevant. The traditional approach to problem-solving seemed futile, and it became clear to me that merely managing the existing system was not enough.

THE TURNING POINT

During a brainstorming session with my team, I was struck by a sudden realization that our fixation on our immediate problems was blinding us to greater possibilities. It was not about fixing what was broken; it was about reimagining what could be. The realization was both exhilarating and terrifying, as it required me to let go of comfortable routines and well-established norms.

I decided then and there to embrace a more visionary mindset, one that looked beyond the immediate challenges and sought opportunities for transformative change. I knew that this shift would not only influence our current situation but would shape my entire approach to leadership, strategy, and organizational growth.

INFLUENCE ON LEADERSHIP

Adopting a visionary mindset has profoundly changed how I lead. Rather than directing from above, I strive to foster a culture where creativity and innovation thrive. I've learned to listen more, ask the right questions, and empower others to explore new horizons. My role became that of an enabler and catalyst for change, rather than a traditional manager.

IMPACT ON STRATEGY

My new approach led to a strategic overhaul within Proshark. We started focusing on long-term goals, recognizing that innovation required more than just quick fixes. We began to invest in research and development, exploring untapped markets, and forming collaborations that would have previously seemed unconventional.

This strategic shift led us to discover new opportunities that were aligned with our core values but were also responsive to the rapidly changing dynamics of our industry. By being willing to take calculated risks, we were able to pivot from a declining path to one filled with potential.

EFFECTS ON ORGANIZATIONAL GROWTH

A visionary mindset is not merely about thinking big; it's about acting big. At Proshark, this approach has fueled exponential growth. By fostering a culture that values innovation and collaboration, we have been able to attract talented individuals who share our vision.

Furthermore, our commitment to strategic innovation has allowed us to create new products and services that resonate with our customers. We've entered new markets and formed partnerships that have significantly expanded our reach.

The growth we've achieved is not just in terms of numbers; it's in the depth of our relationships with our stakeholders, the quality of our offerings, and our reputation as a leader in our field.

The decision to adopt a visionary mindset was not a comfortable one. It required me to challenge my assumptions, take risks, and embrace uncertainty. However, it has been the most rewarding decision of my career.

A visionary approach is not just about seeing the future; it's about shaping it. It's about recognizing that the greatest opportunities often lie beyond the obvious and that real growth requires the courage to venture into the unknown.

This mindset has become the cornerstone of my leadership philosophy and the driving force behind Proshark's success. It has taught me that vision is not a solitary pursuit but a collective endeavor, requiring collaboration, resilience, and a relentless pursuit of excellence.

In a world where change is the only constant, a visionary mindset is not merely an option; it's a necessity. It's what enables us to see beyond the horizon, to envision what's possible, and to build a future that reflects our highest aspirations. For me, it's what leadership is all about.

In the bustling landscape of contemporary business, a CEO must wear many hats. However, one of the most crucial and transformative roles a leader can assume is that of a visionary. Developing a compelling vision is not a mere task but an ongoing process that can shape the very identity and trajectory of an organization. Here's my perspective on how to approach this vital leadership function and how it impacts overall company strategy.

DEVELOPING A COMPELLING VISION

1. **Understanding the Core Values and Purpose**

   A vision is more than a lofty goal or a mission statement. It's an articulation of the company's core values, purpose, and the unique contribution it seeks to make. Identifying and understanding these elements is the foundational step in crafting a vision that resonates.

2. **Engaging Stakeholders**

   A vision cannot be a solitary endeavor; it must be a collective aspiration. Engaging with employees, customers, partners, and other stakeholders can provide insights, align interests, and create a shared sense of ownership.

3. **Looking Beyond the Immediate Horizon**

   A compelling vision requires foresight and the ability to see beyond immediate challenges or opportunities. It's about exploring the larger trends, societal needs, and potential disruptions that may shape the future landscape.

4. **Balancing Ambition with Realism**

   A vision must be bold and inspiring, but it also needs to be grounded in reality. Balancing ambition with an understanding of the capabilities, resources, and constraints can create a vision that is both aspirational and achievable.

5. **Articulating and Communicating the Vision**

   Once crafted, the vision must be articulated in a way that resonates with all stakeholders. It must be communicated consistently and become an integral part of the organizational narrative.

IMPACT ON OVERALL COMPANY STRATEGY

1. **Alignment of Objectives**

   A well-defined vision serves as a guiding star, aligning all strategic objectives and ensuring that short-term goals are consistent with the long-term direction. This alignment creates coherence and synergy across various functions and levels of the organization.

2. **Inspiration and Engagement**

   An inspiring vision can energize and engage employees, fostering a sense of purpose and commitment. It can enhance morale, productivity, and loyalty, creating a culture that is both motivated and aligned.

3. **Influencing Decision Making**

   A clear vision serves as a reference point for decision-making. It helps in evaluating opportunities, assessing risks, and making choices that are consistent with the overall direction of the company.

4. **Enhancing Brand Identity**

   A compelling vision can become a key element of the brand identity, differentiating the organization in the marketplace. It can shape perceptions, build trust, and create emotional connections with customers and partners.

5. **Facilitating Innovation and Agility**

   A visionary approach encourages exploration, innovation, and a willingness to embrace change. It fosters an environment where new ideas are nurtured, and adaptability is valued, enabling the organization to respond to emerging trends and disruptions.

   Developing a compelling vision is both an art and a science. It requires a deep understanding of the organization's essence, an engagement with various stakeholders, a foresight that transcends immediate concerns, and a careful balance between ambition and realism.

The impact of a well-crafted vision goes beyond mere inspiration; it permeates every aspect of the organization's strategy, influencing alignment, decision-making, brand identity, and innovation.

As the CEO of Proshark and CTO of the Strategic Advisor Board, I've seen firsthand how a shared vision can transform a company, galvanizing efforts, aligning interests, and propelling the organization forward. It's not just about where you want to go, but who you want to be, what you want to contribute, and how you want to make a difference.

In the end, a vision is more than a statement; it's a living entity that embodies the soul of an organization. It's the compass that guides, the spark that inspires, and the glue that binds. Crafting it is one of the most profound and rewarding responsibilities of leadership, and its influence can be the defining factor in an organization's success.

In the ever-evolving business landscape, innovation and risk-taking have become synonymous with growth and progress. However, as the CEO of Proshark, I understand that these qualities must be carefully balanced with stability and sustainable growth. Striking this equilibrium is not a simple task but an ongoing challenge that requires careful consideration, strategic planning, and an adaptive mindset. Here's how a visionary CEO can approach this complex but essential endeavor.

1. **Understanding the Essence of Innovation and Risk-taking**

   Firstly, it's important to recognize that innovation and risk-taking are not reckless pursuits. Rather, they are calculated, purpose-driven efforts to explore new horizons, challenge the status quo, and respond to emerging opportunities and threats. They require a willingness to venture into the unknown, but always with a clear understanding of the potential rewards and consequences.

2. **Creating a Culture of Responsible Risk-taking**

   A culture that encourages experimentation but within well-defined boundaries allows employees to explore new ideas without risking the overall stability of the organization. It creates a safe space for creativity, fostering innovation without compromising responsibility.

   Failure is an inherent part of innovation, but it's also an opportunity to learn and grow. By treating failures as learning experiences rather than setbacks, a visionary CEO can build resilience and wisdom within the organization.

3. **Strategic Alignment of Innovation with Organizational Goals**

   Innovation must not be a random or isolated endeavor. It must be aligned with the overall strategy and goals of the organization. By ensuring that innovation efforts are guided by a clear vision and mission, a CEO can maintain a sense of direction and purpose, mitigating unnecessary risks.

4. **Balancing Short-term Gains with Long-term Sustainability**

   Putting all resources into a single innovative project can lead to catastrophic failure. Diversifying investments across different projects, sectors, and stages of development can create a balanced portfolio that fuels innovation while maintaining stability.

Innovation must be pursued with an eye on long-term sustainability. Whether it's environmental, social, or financial sustainability, a responsible approach ensures that growth is not achieved at the expense of future generations or the broader community.

5. **Technology and Data**

   In today's technology-driven world, data analytics and AI can provide insights into market trends, customer behavior, and potential risks. Leveraging these tools enables a visionary CEO to make informed decisions, balancing innovation with calculated risks.

6. **Building Adaptive and Resilient Systems**

   Adaptability and resilience are crucial in an environment where change is constant. Building systems and processes that can respond to emerging challenges or opportunities ensures that the organization can innovate without losing its footing.

7. **Nurturing Leadership at All Levels**

   Encouraging leadership and decision-making at different levels within the organization allows for a more nuanced and diverse approach to innovation and risk management. It creates a distributed network of responsibility and insight, strengthening the organization's ability to balance growth with stability.

   Balancing innovation and risk-taking with stability and sustainable growth is a multifaceted challenge that requires a thoughtful, strategic, and adaptive approach. It's about creating a culture that values creativity but within a framework of responsibility. It's about aligning innovation with strategy, balancing short-term gains with long-term goals, and leveraging technology and leadership to create adaptive and resilient systems.

As the CEO of Proshark and CTO of the Strategic Advisor Board, I've seen how this delicate balance can fuel growth without compromising the foundational principles and values of the organization. It's a dance that requires precision, grace, and a clear understanding of the music – the complex interplay of innovation, risk, stability, and growth.

In the end, being a visionary CEO is not about choosing between innovation and stability; it's about weaving them together into a coherent and resilient tapestry. It's about leading with courage and wisdom, embracing the excitement of discovery while maintaining the serenity of balance. It's a journey that demands both audacity and humility, and it's what makes leadership in today's world both a thrilling adventure and a profound responsibility.

There is no leadership playbook that guarantees success, no formula that can be applied across all situations. However, the tapestry of my career is woven with experiences that reveal the potent impact of visionary leadership. One experience, in particular, stands out, demonstrating how a clear, purpose-driven vision can transform an organization. It's a story that unfolded at Proshark, and the lessons it imparted continue to resonate with me.

THE CHALLENGE AT HAND

Proshark was at a critical juncture, caught between the legacy of our past successes and the uncertainty of a rapidly evolving market. Our once groundbreaking products were beginning to show their age, and competition was mounting. The traditional strategies that had served us well seemed to falter, and the organization was in need of a transformative change.

A Visionary Leap

Recognizing the need for a radical shift, I chose to embark on a path that was both exciting and daunting. The answer was not in merely updating our products or tweaking our marketing strategies; it was in reimagining our very identity and purpose.

We began to look beyond our immediate market, exploring how our core competencies could address broader societal challenges. We shifted our focus from being a technology provider to becoming a catalyst for positive change, leveraging our expertise to create solutions that resonated with emerging global needs.

This was not a decision made in isolation; it involved engaging with our team, our customers, our partners, and even our competitors. It required a willingness to listen, to question, and to challenge our own assumptions.

The Transformation

The shift was not immediate, nor was it without hurdles. However, the clarity of our vision began to permeate the organization, inspiring innovation, fostering collaboration, and aligning our efforts. We invested in research and development, forged new partnerships, and ventured into uncharted territories.

The result was a suite of products and services that not only revitalized our market presence but also redefined our role in the industry. We became leaders in areas we hadn't even considered before, creating value that transcended mere profit.

THE IMPACT

The transformation of Proshark is not merely a story of financial success; it's a testament to the power of visionary leadership. Our vision shaped our strategy, our culture, our relationships, and our very identity. It allowed us to navigate uncertainty, adapt to change, and create a legacy that continues to inspire.

THE LESSONS

Vision Must be Grounded in Purpose: A vision that is rooted in genuine purpose and values resonates deeply, creating alignment and motivation. It's not about chasing trends but understanding what you stand for.

Engagement is Key: A vision is not a monologue but a dialogue. Engaging with various stakeholders ensures that the vision is shared, understood, and embraced.

Courage to Venture into the Unknown: Visionary leadership requires a willingness to take risks and venture into uncharted territories. It's about seeing possibilities where others see barriers.

Flexibility and Adaptability: A vision is not a rigid roadmap but a guiding star. Being flexible and adaptable ensures that you can respond to emerging opportunities and challenges without losing sight of your goals.

Long-term Thinking: Visionary leadership is about playing the long game, understanding that meaningful transformation takes time, effort, and resilience.

The transformation of Proshark is a personal and profound example of how visionary leadership can shape an organization's destiny. It taught me that leadership is not about control but inspiration, not about certainty but exploration, not about power but purpose.

It's an experience that continues to guide my approach as both the CEO of Proshark and the CTO of the Strategic Advisor Board. It reminds me that leadership is not a title but a responsibility, not a position but a journey, not a destination but a continuous process of growth, learning, and contribution.

The lessons gleaned from this experience are not merely theoretical insights but living principles that breathe life into the very essence of leadership. They are reminders that vision is not a luxury but a necessity, a force that can ignite the human spirit, unlock potential, and create a legacy that transcends the ordinary. It's what makes leadership not just a profession but a calling, a craft that shapes not only organizations but lives, communities, and indeed, the very fabric of our world.

In an era where the business landscape is rapidly changing, a growth mindset has become an imperative, not just for individuals but for organizations as a whole. As the CEO of Proshark and CTO of the Strategic Advisor Board, I've come to realize that fostering a culture of continuous learning and improvement is not merely an operational strategy; it's a philosophical commitment to growth, exploration, and excellence. Here's how I believe this can be achieved:

1. **Embracing a Growth Mindset at the Leadership Level**

    The journey towards cultivating a growth mindset within an organization must begin at the top. Leaders must embody the belief that abilities and intelligence can be developed through dedication, hard work, and constructive feedback. It's a mindset that values progress over perfection, curiosity over certainty, and resilience over complacency.

2. **Setting the Tone Through Vision and Values**

   The organizational vision and values must resonate with the principles of growth and learning. They must articulate a commitment to continuous improvement, innovation, collaboration, and adaptability. These guiding principles set the tone and provide a framework within which a growth-oriented culture can flourish.

3. **Investing in Learning and Development**

   Offering ongoing learning opportunities, whether through workshops, online courses, or mentorship programs, fosters a culture where growth is not just encouraged but expected.

   Encouraging collaboration across different functions and teams promotes a culture of shared learning, where diverse perspectives and skills are leveraged for collective growth.

4. **Encouraging Experimentation and Innovation**

   Creating a safe environment where experimentation and innovation are encouraged allows employees to step out of their comfort zones. It promotes a culture where failure is not punished but seen as a valuable learning opportunity.

5. **Implementing Systems for Feedback and Reflection**

   Regular, constructive feedback helps individuals and teams understand their strengths and areas for improvement, fostering a culture where growth is continuous and collaborative.

   Encouraging regular reflection on successes and failures, both at the individual and organizational level, facilitates a deeper understanding of what works and what needs improvement.

6. **Recognizing and Rewarding Growth and Effort**

Acknowledging and rewarding not just outcomes but the effort, progress, collaboration, and learning that led to those outcomes reinforces the importance of growth and continuous improvement.

7. **Leveraging Technology to Facilitate Growth**

    Technology can play a vital role in fostering a growth culture, providing tools for collaboration, learning, analytics, and communication that make growth-oriented practices more accessible and effective.

8. **Promoting Psychological Safety**

    Creating an environment where employees feel safe to express their opinions, ask questions, and challenge prevailing norms is crucial in fostering a culture where learning and growth are intrinsic values.

9. **Leading by Example**

    As a leader, embodying the principles of growth, learning, and continuous improvement is perhaps the most potent way to cultivate these values within the organization. It's about demonstrating through actions and attitudes that growth is not just a priority but a way of life.

    Cultivating a growth mindset and fostering a culture of continuous learning and improvement is a multifaceted endeavor. It requires a conscious effort to shift organizational attitudes, practices, and systems to align with the principles of growth, exploration, and resilience.

    At Proshark, this journey has been both challenging and immensely rewarding. It has transformed our organization into a dynamic, innovative, and responsive entity that thrives on continuous learning and improvement.

The lessons we have learned are not unique to our industry or our organization. They are universal principles that can guide any organization seeking to embrace a growth-oriented culture. They remind us that growth is not a destination but a journey, not a static achievement but a dynamic process, not a solitary pursuit but a collective endeavor.

In a world where change is constant and uncertainty is a given, a growth mindset is not just an advantage; it's a necessity. It's what enables us to navigate complexity with curiosity, face challenges with courage, and turn potential into progress. It's what makes us not just survivors but pioneers, not just participants but creators, not just consumers but contributors.

It's a mindset that sees not just what is but what could be, not just who we are but who we could become. It's a philosophy that shapes not just organizations but lives, not just products but legacies, not just careers but communities. It's the essence of what leadership is and what leadership can be, and it's a journey I invite you all to embark upon.

The role of a CEO is as rewarding as it is demanding. As the head of Proshark and CTO of the Strategic Advisor Board, my days are filled with decisions, challenges, innovations, and constant learning. While the journey has been incredibly fulfilling, it has not been without its share of stress and pressure.

The quest for success and the weight of responsibilities can sometimes overshadow the importance of mental well-being. Yet, over the years, I have learned that taking care of myself mentally, physically, and emotionally is not just a personal necessity; it's a professional one.

UNDERSTANDING THE IMPORTANCE OF MENTAL WELL-BEING

Early in my career, I mistakenly equated long hours and constant work with success. I pushed myself to the brink, often at the expense of my health and relationships. It took a moment of realization and self-reflection to understand that this path was neither sustainable nor healthy.

I began to see that my effectiveness as a leader, my ability to innovate, inspire, and make sound decisions was intricately tied to my mental and physical well-being. I recognized that self-care was not a luxury but a necessity, a vital component of leadership.

DEVELOPING A PERSONALIZED SELF-CARE STRATEGY

1. **Mindfulness and Meditation**

   I have found that starting my day with meditation helps me center myself and approach the day with clarity and calmness. Mindfulness practices have taught me to be present, to respond rather than react, and to approach challenges with equanimity.

2. **Physical Exercise**

   Regular physical exercise has become an essential part of my routine. Whether it's a morning run or a session at the gym, physical activity helps me release stress, energize my body, and clear my mind.

3. **Balanced Nutrition**

   Eating well is not just about physical health; it directly impacts mental well-being. Investing time in preparing balanced meals and enjoying them has become a joyful ritual that nourishes both body and mind.

4. **Time with Loved Ones**

   Spending quality time with family and friends has a grounding effect. It reminds me of what truly matters and provides a support system that is invaluable.

5. **Continuous Learning and Personal Growth**

   Embracing hobbies and continuous learning opportunities allows me to step away from my professional role and explore different facets of myself. Whether it's reading, painting, or attending workshops, these activities stimulate my mind and provide a sense of fulfillment.

6. **Professional Support When Needed**

   Sometimes, professional support from a therapist or coach is essential. It provides an unbiased perspective and tools to navigate complex emotional landscapes.

7. **Time for Reflection**

   Setting aside time for reflection, journaling, and contemplation has helped me understand myself better, recognize patterns, and make conscious choices.

8. **Setting Boundaries**

   Learning to set boundaries and say no when necessary has been a critical aspect of maintaining balance. It's about understanding my limits and respecting them.

LEADING BY EXAMPLE

As a leader, I recognize that my approach to self-care doesn't just affect me; it sets an example for my team. By prioritizing mental well-being, I hope to create a culture where self-care is valued, where balance is not just encouraged but celebrated.

Managing stress and maintaining mental well-being is a continuous journey, one that requires conscious effort, self-awareness, and a willingness to prioritize oneself. It's not a one-size-fits-all approach but a personalized strategy that resonates with one's unique needs and lifestyle.

The practices I have shared have been instrumental in my journey, providing me with the resilience, clarity, and balance needed to navigate the intricate and demanding landscape of entrepreneurship. They have taught me that success is not just about what we achieve but how we achieve it, not just about reaching goals but enjoying the journey, not just about building companies but nurturing ourselves.

In the world of business, where change is constant and challenges are inevitable, taking care of our mental well-being is not just an act of self-preservation; it's an act of leadership. It's what allows us to lead with authenticity, empathy, and wisdom. It's what makes us not just successful entrepreneurs but whole human beings, capable of creating, innovating, and contributing not just to our businesses but to our lives and our communities. It's a lesson I learned through experience, and it's a lesson I hope to share with fellow entrepreneurs and leaders.

In the fast-paced world of technology, the spirit of curiosity and innovation is more than an admirable quality; it's a business imperative. At Proshark, fostering this mindset has been at the core of our growth and success. As someone who's always been fascinated by the power of questions, exploration, and creative thinking, I've tried to instill this curiosity-driven approach within our organization. Here's how we've nurtured it, and the impact it's had on our business:

1. **Cultivating a Culture of Inquiry**

   We encourage everyone at Proshark to ask questions, challenge the status quo, and explore different perspectives. It's not about having all the answers but about having the courage to ask the right questions.

We have cultivated an environment where failure isn't a dead-end but a stepping stone towards success. By viewing failure as a learning opportunity, we allow our team to experiment and innovate without the fear of judgment or repercussion.

2. **Investing in Continuous Learning**

   From workshops to conferences, we invest in continuous learning opportunities to fuel curiosity. We support initiatives that allow our employees to learn new skills, technologies, and methodologies.

   We encourage collaboration across different departments. Diverse teams foster innovation by bringing various perspectives and expertise to the table.

3. **Encouraging Autonomy and Ownership**

   Empowering our team members to take ownership of their projects cultivates a sense of responsibility and creativity. It promotes initiative and enables individuals to pursue ideas they are passionate about.

4. **Implementing Innovation Labs and Hackathons**

   We frequently organize internal innovation labs and hackathons to ignite the spark of creativity. These initiatives allow our team to step out of their daily routines and work on projects that inspire them.

5. **Leveraging Technology**

   We utilize cutting-edge technology not just to enhance our products but also to foster innovation. Tools that facilitate collaboration, experimentation, and analysis support our team in bringing their creative ideas to fruition.

6. **Leading by Example**

   As a leader, I strive to model the mindset I want to see in our organization. I make it a point to stay curious, continuously learn, and be open to new ideas and perspectives.

7. **Rewarding Innovation and Curiosity**

   Recognizing and rewarding innovative efforts is crucial in reinforcing the importance of curiosity and creativity. It's about celebrating not just success but the innovative thinking and relentless effort behind it.

IMPACT ON BUSINESS GROWTH

This culture of curiosity has significantly accelerated our innovation process. It has led to groundbreaking products, solutions, and strategies that have set us apart in the market.

By fostering a mindset that values different perspectives and collaborative exploration, we have enhanced the synergy within our teams. This has led to more effective problem-solving and product development.

A curious mindset enables us to adapt to changes swiftly. Whether it's a market shift or technological advancement, our ability to question, learn, and adapt has made us resilient and agile.

Our culture of curiosity and innovation has not only helped us retain our top talent but also attract like-minded individuals. It's become a defining feature of who we are as a company.

Fostering a sense of curiosity and innovation is not a one-off initiative but a continual effort. It's about building a culture that lives and breathes curiosity, where innovation is not a department but a way of thinking, where creativity is not an exception but an expectation.

At Proshark, this approach has been instrumental in our growth, helping us stay ahead of the curve and resonate with our clients and community. It's taught us that true innovation is not just about technology or products but about people and their ability to explore, question, create, and reimagine.

In an ever-evolving business landscape, curiosity and innovation are not just desirable qualities; they are essential to survival and success. They enable us not just to navigate the present but to envision and shape the future. They remind us that in business, as in life, it's not just about reaching destinations but about enjoying and learning from the journey.

At Proshark, we continue to embrace this journey, knowing that our curiosity and creativity are our most valuable assets, not just for growth but for fulfillment, not just for profit but for purpose, not just for building a company but for contributing to a world that's continually learning, growing, and evolving.

Leadership, particularly at the CEO level, requires a blend of skills, attitudes, and behaviors that evolve with experience, demands, and goals. Over the years, I have consciously cultivated habits and daily routines to maintain and enhance my CEO mindset. These practices are not just about productivity but about purpose, alignment, resilience, and growth.

1. **Structured Morning Routine**

    I believe that the way you start your day significantly impacts the rest of it. My morning routine includes meditation, exercise, and a healthy breakfast. This grounding ritual sets the tone, energizes my body, and clears my mind for the day ahead.

2. **Continuous Learning**

The business landscape is always shifting, and staying ahead means continuous learning. Every day, I dedicate time to reading, whether it's industry reports, books, or articles. It keeps me informed, sparks creativity, and fuels my growth mindset.

3. **Time Management and Prioritization**

   I've developed a habit of carefully planning my day, setting clear priorities and goals. I also ensure that I have blocks of uninterrupted time for strategic thinking and vital tasks. This practice keeps me focused and aligned with my broader objectives.

4. **Regular Reflection and Goal Setting**

   Reflection is an integral part of my routine. I set aside time weekly to assess my progress, reflect on my actions, and adjust my strategies as needed. It enables me to be agile and adaptable in my leadership approach.

5. **Cultivating Relationships**

   I make it a priority to connect with my team members, peers, and mentors regularly. Building and maintaining these relationships is not just about networking but about mutual growth, support, and collaboration.

6. **Emphasizing Health and Well-being**

   Being a CEO is demanding, and maintaining optimal health is paramount. My daily routine includes proper nutrition, regular exercise, and sufficient sleep. I also practice mindfulness to ensure mental well-being.

7. **Encouraging Creativity and Innovation**

   Every day, I strive to foster an environment where ideas can flourish. Whether it's brainstorming sessions, collaborative projects, or innovation labs, I actively participate in creative endeavors to stimulate my own thinking and support my team.

8. **Practicing Gratitude**

I've found that the practice of gratitude enhances my perspective and resilience. Taking moments to acknowledge and appreciate successes, even small ones, fosters positivity and motivation.

9. **Balancing Work and Personal Life**

   Work-life balance is essential for sustained performance. I ensure that I spend quality time with family and engage in hobbies that refresh and inspire me. It keeps me grounded and rejuvenated.

10. **Embracing Failure and Learning from Mistakes**

    I have made it a practice to view failures and mistakes as learning opportunities. By analyzing them and extracting lessons, I continually refine my strategies and grow as a leader.

11. **Being Authentic and Transparent**

    I strive to lead with authenticity and transparency, creating a culture of trust and openness. This habit has translated into stronger relationships, better collaboration, and a more aligned organization.

12. **Staying Connected to the Company's Mission and Values**

    Regularly revisiting our mission and values ensures alignment and purpose in my actions and decisions. It serves as a guiding compass in the fast-paced and complex world of business.

    These habits and daily routines are not just practices but principles that guide my leadership journey. They are not static but evolve with me, reflecting my growth, goals, and the ever-changing landscape of business. They remind me that being a CEO is not just about leading a company but leading oneself, not just about achieving targets but nurturing growth, not just about managing others but inspiring them.

At Proshark, these principles have not only shaped my leadership but have permeated our organizational culture. They have helped us navigate challenges with resilience, approach opportunities with curiosity, and build a company that is not just successful but meaningful.

I believe that the CEO mindset is not a fixed trait but a cultivated perspective. It's about creating a harmony between the professional and personal, the strategic and the empathetic, the bold and the mindful. It's about recognizing that leadership is not a destination but a journey, one that demands continuous reflection, learning, adaptation, and, most importantly, a willingness to grow not just as a leader but as a human being.

In the rapidly evolving world of business, aspiring leaders must equip themselves with a mindset that not only embraces change but thrives on it. Developing a visionary mindset and strategic thinking capabilities has been instrumental in my journey, and I believe they are essential for any emerging leader. Here are my insights and advice for those looking to cultivate these qualities:

1. **Embrace a Growth Mindset**

   Keep asking questions, explore new territories, and don't be afraid to challenge the status quo. Curiosity will fuel your innovative thinking and broaden your horizons.

   Commit to learning new skills, technologies, and industry trends. Stay updated and engaged in your field, and don't hesitate to venture into areas outside your comfort zone.

2. **Develop a Clear Vision**

   Understanding your purpose and aligning it with your values will guide your decision-making process and keep you focused on long-term goals.

Create a vivid picture of what success looks like for you and your organization. Share it with your team, so they can align their efforts towards a common goal.

3. **Foster Resilience and Adaptability**

   Don't shy away from failure. Analyze your mistakes, learn from them, and use them as stepping stones towards success.

   Adaptability is key in a fast-paced environment. Be ready to pivot when necessary and make strategic adjustments as you learn and grow.

4. **Encourage Collaboration and Diverse Thinking**

   Surround yourself with people who bring different perspectives, skills, and backgrounds. Encourage open communication and value every voice.

   Find mentors who can guide you and offer valuable insights. Equally, be a mentor to others; teaching can also be a powerful learning tool.

5. **Focus on Long-term Strategic Thinking**

   Develop the ability to analyze complex situations, identify patterns, and anticipate future trends. This foresight is crucial for strategic planning.

   While immediate results are important, keep an eye on the long-term vision. Every decision should be a step towards your ultimate objectives.

6. **Cultivate Emotional Intelligence**

   Understand the needs and perspectives of your team and stakeholders. Emotional intelligence enhances your leadership skills and builds stronger relationships.

   Learn to recognize and manage your emotions, especially under pressure. Emotional balance will support your decision-making process.

7. **Lead with Authenticity**

Embrace your unique strengths and weaknesses. Authentic leadership resonates with people and fosters trust.

Clear, honest communication is vital in building confidence and alignment within your team.

8. **Reflect and Adjust Regularly**

Set regular intervals to assess your progress, reflect on your actions, and adjust your strategies as needed.

Acknowledge achievements, both big and small. It fosters motivation and a positive culture.

The journey towards becoming a visionary leader with strategic thinking capabilities is a continuous process of growth, learning, and adaptation. It's not a linear path but a dynamic, exciting adventure filled with challenges, discoveries, failures, and successes.

Remember, visionary leadership is not just about seeing the future but shaping it. It's about inspiring others to join you on a journey towards something greater, something meaningful. It's about having the courage to dream big and the wisdom to navigate the intricate path towards those dreams.

At Proshark, our visionary approach has been a driving force behind our success. I encourage you to embrace this mindset, apply these principles, and embark on your unique leadership journey. Believe in yourself, stay curious, be resilient, and most importantly, never stop learning and growing.

The world needs visionary leaders who are not just prepared for the future but are excited to create it. Be that leader. The path is yours to shape.

ABOUT THE AUTHOR

A seasoned entrepreneur, Joel is CEO and founder of Proshark as well as founder, CTO, and Global Managing Partner of the Strategic Advisor Board. He has extensive experience in leadership, innovation, software development, automation, app development, data sciences, analytics, cybersecurity, and real estate.

He serves on multiple boards and believes the next step in technological evolution brings the convergence of blockchain, artificial intelligence, augmented reality, and data sciences.

- Member of Mensa, Bellwether, and ACA
- Licensed Real Estate Broker with commercial development experience
- Resume includes 4G Development, Sony Pictures Digital Entertainment, eAssist Global Solutions, and American Loans
- Volunteer work includes J Ryley Foundation, Habitat for Humanity, and Planning Commission Chairman
- Hobbies include flying, sailing, golfing, biking, music, and music production

VISIONARY LEADERSHIP AND ADAPTABILITY

MICHAEL SIPE

There is a perception that CEOs today need to be visionary, and that's true. But a CEO also needs what we call traditional characteristics. Today's business world is changing much more quickly in many industries. Technology changes often, but when you look closely, technological changes grow exponentially following the rate of Moore's law. That's quick! Companies in quickly evolving markets or technology-dependent companies must adapt to the change, or they won't survive.

We've seen a more traditional leadership style for industries that are slower to change, with some needing to adapt. And in the fast-paced trend-change industries, adaptability is a more prevalent skill yet a classic characteristic that has been around for decades. Adaptability is a skill of conventional leadership. But not anticipating trend changes, especially in today's faster-paced world across all industries, can leave a company flat-footed and ill-prepared for change. That's where CEOs today need to be more visionary.

Visionary leaders need to think and plan strategically in a way that anticipates changes in trends and opportunities for growth. The problem often faced by visionary CEOs is they fail the company as a visionary leader. What happens is that the positive impact of innovative leadership breaks down when middle managers aren't aligned with top management's strategic vision. Creative leaders need to incorporate practices that are traditional management techniques and characteristics. The CEOs need to have senior management understand the strategic vision and direction. Then they must create strategic alignment among middle managers before strategy execution efforts begin. They must clearly articulate how middle management supports and contributes directly to the strategic vision. It is a communication exercise that high-performing, traditional CEOs have had as a characteristic.

Suppose they don't do a communication translation of the idea to middle management. In that case, middle management keeps doing what they have always done because that's what they know, and that's how their performance and production have traditionally been evaluated. They will resist change. It makes sense then that visionary CEOs today have the vision to adapt quicker. Still, they must leverage the skill sets of successful traditional CEOs of effective communication across all management layers. That way, visionary CEOs of today can be both strategic and effective in execution to be ahead of the rapidly changing world.

As a military leader, I have been to some of the best schools and training to learn advanced management techniques, leadership methods, and styles. I had become an effective leader inspiring those under me in the organization to perform better and produce more. It was rewarding to see the teamwork and collaborative culture. Yet, as a senior manager or executive in my organizations, I found that a rogue wave of unanticipated change often came and knocked my organizations and me significantly off track. It created confusion, uncertainty, and stress, resulting in a lack of collaboration.

We could adapt to more minor, unanticipated changes. But these more significant changes were debilitating and threatening. After going through several challenges in various careers, organizations, and positions of command in CEO and CEO-like positions, I decided I needed to figure out how to best prepare for unexpected changes.

I discovered that many of the rogue waves weren't all that rogue. Sure, one might not have been able to predict that COVID would break out and majorly impact everyone globally. But one could have anticipated that some worldwide virus outbreak could or would happen. The more I dug into what was possible, I began to see trends. Specifically, there was almost a predictability to disruptive trends across virtually any business, government, or society.

If one could identify trends, one could begin to predict the significant elements of trend changes and, most importantly, prepare for the disruption or find and embrace to be best positioned for the disruption. If a business leader could identify opportunities to disrupt a stale trend, they could gain a market advantage or be the most adept and innovative leader. That means having a vision for how and when changes would affect their organization or market.

I had the opportunity to apply this knowledge as the senior advisor to the strategic capabilities division of a multibillion-dollar organization. I had to identify and evaluate which new technologies could be disruptive and determine which ones would have the greatest likelihood of succeeding in the marketplace as a disruptor that would effectively and efficiently change trends dramatically.

After seeing and evaluating potential disruptors, I learned that most people have an inherent instinct or intuition to know what defines a disruptor. The problem was that there was a mindset of accepting the status quo. But if a leader can tap into their imagination or show their subordinates how to use it, that instinct would kick in, and they could see the impact. They would have some vision of what was possible through innovation or anticipating trend changes.

Leveraging instinct and intuition became a requirement to be visionary. I learned to incorporate creative practice as a leader. That practice enabled me to forecast impactful change or to take advantage of opportunities to make disruptive changes that would benefit the organization or society.

A CEO needs to understand and articulate the organization's mission. They need to answer who they serve, what they do, how they do it, and, most importantly, why. When a CEO understands the "why" the organization does what they do, it creates a sense of purpose. That sense of purpose takes a CEO's focus from being in work myopically. It changes the direction to a broader expansive focus on impact—a CEO who knows their company's actions can then define impactful goals, and they can sense when those impacts are being appropriately served for growth or impacted by the change, both internally and externally.

Case in point: Large, multinational companies that have been around for decades have seen their workforce demographics dramatically change. Those changes are part of a trend. Likewise, technological advances are an external factor that can impact a company significantly. A CEO who knows the company's impact must look at internal and external factors and trends that will alter a company's more significant effect. A CEO who can anticipate external and internal influences is using their visionary skills. In turn, they then assess the results on their company's ability to execute its purpose and impact overall. That assessment is used to formulate a strategy for both survival and growth. The vision of knowing the effect of strategic internal and external factors and the complementary approach to prepare, adapt to, and leverage them is essential for business success.

There is a solid human desire and emphasis in today's fast-paced world to be creative and innovative. CEOs and business leaders are told to embrace change and be ahead of trend changes. If innovation becomes an obsession without the necessary guidelines, it becomes a proclivity to take on excess risk. The policies that are necessary when a company innovates and takes on risk with the innovation are not constrictive but supportive. As a former director of innovation at a disruptive technology organization, I saw many impressive and fascinating new technologies and techniques. Each innovative technology or technique had people that were both responsible for its creation but also for promoting the innovation.

There are human tendencies to inspiration and creativity. Being in a state of imagination and creativity can be a strong, powerful energetic force. It can be fun and exhilarating. People become enthusiastic and attached to their creative ideas and projects. While that attachment evokes support and contribution, it can make people overzealous or blind to potential shortfalls. Innovation by itself may not be risky, but how it is used and implemented can induce risk, and sometimes considerable risk if subconsciously or consciously ignored. That's why guidelines should be in place to assess and mitigate risk when implementing innovation.

Here are a few guidelines a CEO should consider:

What is the impact of implementing invention on resources? Specifically, what is the time and financial cost of labor and materials? Once those are identified, how much cost to capital and lowering revenue while being developed and implemented does the endeavor have? Each company has some, if only a few, revenue streams. Innovation that takes up many resources and affects a large percentage of revenue is more impactful for the company. More people are directly and indirectly involved and attached to the outcome of the innovation endeavor. That means workforce production for existing revenue can be adversely impacted if workforce allocation is suboptimal to continue the existing income. I've seen this often where companies get so engrossed in innovation that they neglect their current duties and obligations to sustain those existing revenue sources. A proper resource impact assessment is the first guideline. That way, a CEO and the management team can allocate the appropriate resources to the innovation endeavor without extending the company.

Don't get complacent with the status quo. Often, a company can get into a success pattern with its existing product or service lines. Human nature likes predictability, and a tendency to accept company output as an expected event comes with that. The expectation will inevitably be affected by an internal or external change. A visionary CEO and management team need some innovation to stay ahead of trend changes or to continually have fresh ideas that will add to the growth and scaling of the company in the marketplace.

Create a company culture that encourages innovation at all levels. This has a beneficial twofold effect. The CEO will only be able to anticipate some changes coming to the company. Having a company culture that is creative, imaginative, and resourceful will be much more likely to see the impact of change before it happens and warn the company. The second effect is that more creative and innovative ideas will be considered instead of just coming from the CEO. A company CEO who creates and encourages an innovative culture with risk mitigation guidelines has a dynamic and responsive company that will grow quicker, faster, and more adroitly in the marketplace.

When I was in charge of a billion-dollar joint venture project comprised of disparate companies that each had a technology or service that made a potent capability, it struggled during the early phases of development. There were four major components, and different organizations owned each. Individually, these components were impressive technologies and innovative in their own right. But put together, they would make something truly remarkable and be a significant disruptor for the customer.

We put in place appropriate systems and procedures for project management of development. Despite the methods and techniques, people were people. Some teams needed deadlines, others needed to be collaborating, and it was getting quite frustrating as we fell behind on our timeline. Most importantly, I sensed there wasn't an uplifting quality of energy the people possessed. While it may seem obvious in hindsight, at the time, I kept trying to lead and fix things using best practices of the empowering style of leadership.

One day, I realized I knew more about the overall effect and impact the final product would have than anyone else. I knew what its true potential was. Yet, I hadn't articulated it well to all the teams. I had the expanded vision for its glorious use and impact and made the mistake of assuming that everyone had the same macro idea I did. Parts of the effects just seemed obvious. That wasn't the problem. I realized some other parts were less than apparent, and it was because not everyone in a management position had the experience and perspective I did.

A reputable leader possesses the ability to inspire and motivate. How they do it is unique because many effective methods and styles are used today. One of the methods is to communicate the vision and its impact to subordinates. It creates a sense of purpose because they know their input is essential to the project's success, if not vital.

I realized I hadn't done a thorough job explaining the impact of the overall capability and how each major component and the corresponding organization contributed to its success in executing the vision. I called a meeting and reviewed with each of the teams present at the conference how each component required integration, complemented each other, and was necessary for the overall effectiveness of more potent capability. By the end of the meeting, each team's management understood how they contributed to the overall project. Most importantly, they understood how their components were essential to executing the grander vision. From that point on, the project went much more smoothly because everyone knew what the concept was, how we would get there, and why their addition was vital to the execution of the vision.

A CEO can cultivate a growth mindset by starting with themselves. Every leader who is respected and admired has followers looking for guidance. One of the best ways to lead is to set an example. Setting the benchmark of continuous personal learning and growth shows followers how to act and behave in a way that promotes a growth mindset.

But a growth mindset isn't just a personal or professional development aspect. A growth mindset is also one whereby an organization grows financially, emotionally, and intelligently. Increasing revenue is one financial component; growing assets is another. It requires a mindset of leaders and followers to implement a system that generates economic growth. A CEO needs to instill an expectation for financial gain that the company embraces because that financial expectation and how to execute it has been communicated to inspire a desire for growth.

Another component of company growth is emotional intelligence, which refers to the ability of an individual or a collective of people to identify and express emotional understanding. A company with a higher, more elevated emotional intelligence can adapt to stressors and create solutions rather than blame others, avoid the problem because of being offended, or not contributing when needed. Emotionally strong companies look to solve issues and withstand challenges together because they possess great wisdom and emotional intelligence that uplifts and restores each other. Emotional growth mindsets encourage and support each other to execute goals. Each individual who leans into participating in the organization will be emotionally invested and learn from others how to handle challenges more effectively emotionally.

The third component of a growth mindset is the learning component that contributes to gaining intelligence and wisdom. Experience can be one of the most excellent methods for learning and growing intelligence. When individuals or companies learn from their choices that didn't go as planned, they gain the opportunity from experience to do it differently next time. When they do it differently and get better results, they are executing a wiser intelligence from deciding to use the experience as a learning moment. When CEOs, management, and employees see experiences as learning moments, they inherently build and strengthen a critical component of a growth mindset. Each action an individual or collective takes has a consequence. A growth mindset sees that each result presents an opportunity to learn and grow from the experience.

I simplify the mental well-being process because when significant or moderate stressors come to one's personal experience, it typically overwhelms one to the point of being unclear about how to respond. Some simple practices make remembering easier in the heat of the moment or during overwhelming stress. The first step is to be aware of your reaction to the situation. We often get so caught up in the moment that we can't think straight or act normally, and our response is primarily subconscious. If we can consciously become aware of the cause and effect of stress, we are ready to take the next step.

The second step is to make a choice. Do we want to respond the way we are responding to the stress, or do we want to answer a certain way as we have in the past? When you realize you have a choice in how to react, you can choose a method of dealing with stress that is unique and aligned best with where you are in that very experience. For me, when I get to the point where I can make a choice, I choose to use the following technique: I like to slow down my breathing and focus on my heart area. By slowing down the breathing and focusing on my breath as if it is going in and out of the heart region of my chest, I am centering my attention on the part of the body that is very powerful and restorative.

What happens is that the brain and all the stressful thoughts diminish, and the heart becomes the dominant force providing healthy and restorative signals to the brain. The brain, in turn, harmonizes into a more alpha brain wave state and sends information signals to the body that release chemicals that calm and restore. We bring the brain into coherence with the heart. When we are under stress, our brain goes into a distorted beta brain wave state that turns on the sympathetic nervous system used primarily for fight or flight. That's a system that is only needed occasionally. The rest of the time, our body should be governed by the parasympathetic nervous system, which sends that restorative programming chemically to the body.

Practicing heart coherence for a few minutes daily is a healthy way to handle stress. I meditate for an hour or more each morning to get into that alpha and theta brain wave state. It's good for the body and clears up the distortive thinking I can get sucked into doing. It trains the mind and body into an expansive and more aware consciousness. It utilizes and exercises different parts of the brain, which can be accessed and used later in the day. It helps me be more creative and inventive and adapt to environmental changes. Any CEO who wants to be more adaptable, insightful, and inspiring can use a meditative practice to enhance those capabilities.

I enjoy listening and learning from Simon Sinek. He is most known for asking the question, "Why?" When we were little kids, we didn't understand many things that happened in the world. We had an innate curiosity and often asked why things happened the way they did or why they were the way they were. As people grew older, they typically stopped asking as many questions from a curiosity perspective. They learned because they had a personally developed objective and less from a place of curiosity.

For example, they wanted a specific degree from college to do well in a specialized profession. Most often, it was not because it was so intriguing and that they were overly curious but because it would generate a better financial experience. That reasoning mindset overrides the inquisitiveness and spontaneity of wondering why people do what they do or why things happen the way they do.

To foster a sense of curiosity as an adult and in your company, it is essential to value and support employee creativity. Encouraging them to think outside the norms and creatively provide potential solutions to company problems causes them to ponder and reflect on the issue. Inevitably, they will ask themselves or others in the company, "Why do or did things happen that way?" Collectively, we are wiser than we are individually, and a curious collective will be much quicker at finding solutions to problems when they are encouraged to be involved in the minor and major challenges their company faces.

I have found in my companies that when I look at challenges with curiosity instead of a view of frustration, I am much more likely to identify a solution. I'm turning on the parasympathetic rather than the sympathetic nervous system. I'm in a more expansive state of mind and consciousness when doing this, which has been immensely beneficial. I'm often amazed that when a group does the same thing, they get different perspectives from that curiosity and come up with solutions that may not work but that trigger another person in the group to leap to another solution that does work. Building a team that naturally embraces and exudes collaborative curiosity drives the sparks of innovation and adaptability, which are essential for a company's growth.

I mentioned earlier that I meditate in the morning and do this in other forms before I go to bed in the evening. The evening practice of meditatively winding down enables you to fall asleep more easily. Much research proves that getting between seven and nine hours of sleep help with cognition and the ability to be more resilient to stressors.

My evening meditation practice sets me up for success in getting the seven or eight hours of sleep my body needs. I wake up naturally and effortlessly, whereas when I didn't have that practice, I would begrudgingly wake up to an unwanted alarm and become annoyed, which would trigger me to start thinking about everything I had to do that day. I bookend my days with a mentally and physiologically healthy restorative, rejuvenating practice that fosters the creative capacity of expanded consciousness. During the day, I exercise and implement some heart and brain coherence breathing exercises.

One of my other favorite practices is using a community support network. A supportive community can be just two people, a family, a spouse, some close friends, colleagues from work, a mentorship organization, a business coach, or professional organizations that uplift and inspire. When we exchange our thoughts, emotions, and desires with others, we share and ask for support. We get to give and get a form of love when we engage with these communities we surround ourselves with.

It's essential to surround yourself with like-minded and vibrational thought people we want to be or continue to be like. That provides us with the model of energy and enthusiasm that uplifts and inspires more excellent performance and healthy being. I enjoy surfing, and I love that community because there is a stoke from surfing, and most surfers experiencing the uplifting stoke are a fun and supportive group of people. Exercise and camaraderie are combined into one activity that can energize you.

I recommend nine steps to develop your visionary mindset and strategic thinking as a CEO and leader:

1. Watch and guard your thoughts and emotions (meditation, prayer, yoga, etc.).

2. Ask why your company, marketplace, and environments are how they are.

3. Encourage creativity and create a culture of curiosity and desire by problem-solving from top to bottom in your company.

4. Surround yourself with the kind of people that will encourage your growth and inspire you.

5. Get a coach or mentor to promote your personal and professional development.

6. Put guidelines in place for encouraging but wisely incorporating a group mindset of innovation with risk mitigation.

7. Identify trends and ask how they could be improved or why they would change.

8. Use the trend insights to create a strategy that can adapt to imminent and long-term trends or develop capabilities to disrupt and improve market trends.

9. Communicate why and how the strategies are to be implemented in a relevant way to all levels of management.

In this chapter, I have examined a CEO's multi-faceted role in cultivating a company's growth mindset. The key insight is that a growth mindset is not just an individual trait but can be systematically fostered at all levels of an organization. A visionary CEO sets the tone for innovation and strategic thinking and creates a culture that values curiosity, emotional intelligence, and continuous learning. By taking a holistic approach—from setting a compelling vision to fostering emotional intelligence to establishing policies to mitigate risk in innovation—the leader ensures that the company is adaptive and proactive in an ever-changing business environment.

However, the journey doesn't end in the boardroom or shop floor. Personal practices such as meditation and community engagement enrich a CEO's emotional and intellectual toolkit, enabling them to bring their best selves to their challenging role. This 'inside-out' approach to leadership is a cornerstone to building companies that are resilient, innovative, and committed to their core purpose. By integrating these elements into their daily lives and actions, CEOs and their teams are better equipped to meet the complex challenges and opportunities of the future and grow financially, emotionally, and intellectually.

ABOUT THE AUTHOR

Michael is a leadership and life expert who helps audiences learn about the secrets to life and building a stronger, resilient culture of community at work and at home. As a former Navy pilot instructor who frequently overcame the fear of death while training students to land on aircraft carriers at night, Michael regales audiences with harrowing and unusual sea-stories. Each story shares a life or business lesson that addresses some of the most challenging moments people have today. Audiences feel connected at a deep, meaningful level and walk away with best practices for personal, professional, and group development. Michael serves as a business and life coach with a passion to help create abundance in business and in one's personal life so that one has a harmonious work/life balance. Michael has trained, coached, and mentored thousands of people for over three decades.

Michael is the owner of Sipe Coaching and Consulting and an owner/director at The Strategic Advisor Board, a small and mid-tier business consulting firm comprised of ten business owners themselves who help guide small business entrepreneurs to rapid growth using their 100+ years of experience. He is a 5x international bestselling author and bestselling published author with his current book, *Out of Dad's Box: How to Break Free from Overly Controlling Parents and Transform Your Life at Any Age.*

Unleashing Visionary Leadership Through Communication

Patricia Baronowski-Schneider

A visionary CEO is someone who has a clear and compelling vision for the future of their organization. They can see beyond the present and imagine what is possible. They can also articulate this vision to others and inspire them to share it. Unlike traditional CEOs, who focus on maintaining the status quo, visionary leaders embrace change and innovation as the lifeblood of their company. In today's dynamic business landscape, where disruption is the norm, these qualities are vital for staying relevant and seizing emerging opportunities. Visionary CEOs possess an innate ability to anticipate industry shifts, predict market trends, and envision a future that transcends current boundaries. This foresight enables them to chart strategic courses that propel their organizations to new heights.

Traditional CEOs, on the other hand, are more focused on the day-to-day operations of their businesses. They are good at managing the status quo but may need to improve at thinking outside the box and developing new ideas. In today's business world, visionary leadership is essential. The pace of change is accelerating, and businesses need to be able to adapt quickly to survive. Visionary CEOs can see emerging trends and opportunities and make the necessary business changes.

My own visionary mindset has influenced my approach to leadership, strategy, and organizational growth in several ways:

First, it has helped me set ambitious goals for the company. I always look for ways to grow the business and achieve new heights.

Second, my visionary mindset has helped me make bold decisions. I am unafraid to take risks (as seen from my previous fifteen-year skydiving side-hustle career) and always willing to try new things.

Third, my visionary mindset has helped me inspire others. I can share my vision with others and motivate them to work toward it.

A compelling vision is clear, concise, and inspiring. It should be something that people can rally around and believe in. There are a few steps that a CEO can take to develop a compelling vision for their organization:

Start by understanding the current state of the organization. What are the organization's strengths and weaknesses? What opportunities and threats does it face?

Think about the future of the industry. What are the trends that are emerging? What are the available opportunities?

Brainstorm a few different visions for the organization. What could the organization be like in the future? What would it achieve?

Choose the vision that is the most compelling and inspiring. This is the vision that will motivate people to work toward it. Once the vision has been developed, it must be communicated to the rest of the organization. The vision should be something that everyone can understand and rally around. The vision should also be used to guide the company's strategy. The strategy should be aligned with the vision, and it should be designed to achieve the vision.

Balancing innovation and risk-taking with stability and sustainable growth is a delicate balancing act. A visionary CEO needs to see the opportunities for innovation and be aware of the risks involved. There are a few things that a visionary CEO can do to balance innovation and risk-taking with stability and sustainable growth:

Start by understanding the organization's risk tolerance. How much risk is the organization willing to take?

Develop a risk-management plan. This plan should identify the risks involved in innovation and how they will be mitigated.

Create a culture of innovation. This culture should encourage people to take risks and try new things.

Measure the results of innovation. This will help the organization determine which innovations are successful and which aren't.

One personal experience that demonstrates the impact of visionary leadership on an organization's success is when I was working as a marketing manager for a small software company. The company struggled to compete with larger competitors, and I knew we needed to do something different. I started to think about the software industry's future and realized there was a massive opportunity for businesses to use the Internet to reach new customers. I shared my vision with the CEO, and we decided to pivot the company's business model. We started developing software allowing businesses to sell their products and services online. We were one of the first companies to do this, and it was a huge success. The company snowballed, and we became one of the leading software companies in the world. This experience taught me the importance of having a visionary mindset. The company would have failed if I had not seen the software industry's future.

The lessons that can be learned from this experience are:

- Visionary leadership is essential for success in today's business world
- Leaders need to see the future and imagine what is possible
- Leaders need to be able to articulate their vision to others and inspire them to share it
- Leaders need to be willing to take risks and try new things

A growth mindset believes hard work and effort can develop intelligence and abilities. A CEO can cultivate a growth mindset within their organization by:

- Emphasizing the importance of learning and development
- Creating opportunities for employees to learn and grow
- Rewarding employees for taking risks and trying new things
- Creating a culture of feedback and support

A continuous learning and improvement culture encourages employees to learn new things and constantly improve their skills and knowledge. This culture can be fostered by:

- Creating a learning environment where employees feel comfortable taking risks and trying new things

- Providing employees with access to training and development opportunities
- Celebrating successes and learning from failures

Managing stress and maintaining mental well-being as an entrepreneur can be challenging. However, there are a few things that I have found to be helpful:

- Setting boundaries between work and personal life. This is sometimes easier said than done, but it's essential.
- Making time for relaxation and activities that I enjoy. It's easy to get caught up working seven days a week or sixteen-plus hours a day—but that leads to burnout and mental exhaustion, neither of which serves us.
- Getting enough sleep
- Eating a healthy diet
- Exercising regularly
- Practicing mindfulness and meditation

The self-care practices that have been most effective for me are:

Meditation. I meditate for twenty minutes daily. This helps me to relax, focus, and clear my mind. And I don't mean that I sit and meditate customarily. To me, it is a matter of relaxing. Take a few minutes to regroup—gather my thoughts and think about what matters most. I wish you could see my walls. I have photos of my kids, grandkids, husband, family, sunrises, and sunsets—even my skydiving photos (as that was a major relaxing time for me) all around my desk. I take time each day to stare at the photos and think of all the good in front of me. That is my sort-of meditation each day: de-stressing, relaxing, focusing on what is important to me, and starting fresh.

Exercise. I exercise for 30–60 minutes most days of the week. This helps me to reduce stress, improve my mood, and boost my energy levels. It doesn't have to be a chore, either. I always tape all my favorite shows, which lets me stay focused on my treadmill, where I am not paying attention to the task. Instead, I am intrigued by what is on television. I was so fascinated watching a movie once that I maxed out the time allowed for a session on the treadmill. I wasn't running on it like a race, but walking very fast, and I was so engrossed in the movie that after three hours, it stopped.

Reading. I read for at least thirty minutes every day. This helps me to relax and escape from the stresses of life.

Spending time in nature. I try to spend time in nature every day. This helps me to connect with the present moment and appreciate the beauty of the world around me. Even if I can't physically be in nature, I watch pictures and videos of nature online, which sets my mood to a more relaxing tune.

Fostering a culture of curiosity and innovation is paramount to driving sustainable business growth. As a visionary CEO, I encourage an environment where employees are empowered to question conventions, challenge assumptions, and explore uncharted territories. We hold regular brainstorming sessions, cross-functional collaborations, and innovation challenges that stimulate creative thinking. We create a fertile ground for breakthrough ideas by celebrating diverse perspectives and encouraging risk-taking. This approach fuels product and service innovation and inspires a dynamic workplace that attracts top talent and keeps us at the forefront of industry trends.

I also foster a sense of curiosity and innovation within my company by:

- Encouraging employees to ask questions and challenge the status quo.

- Providing employees with opportunities to experiment and try new things. This often brings out some of the most substantial outcomes.
- Celebrating successes and learning from failures. I hate even using the word *failure* because it's a learning experience. If we tried something and it didn't work, well, now we learned what *not* to do and continue ahead until we find what works best.
- Creating a culture of feedback and support. That is so important. If someone assumes what they are doing is excellent, yet it is technically not, how else would they know to choose a different method? If someone is not doing something because they think it won't work or think it's not a good thing, how else can we steer them toward taking a chance and reap the reward of the success if we don't give them this feedback? Whenever someone gives me feedback—praise or constructive criticism—it is valuable and helps me, like a child guided by our parents. That is how we grow, no matter the position, the title, or the job.

Feedback and support are fundamental. This mindset has influenced my business growth in several ways:

First, it has helped me to attract and retain top talent.

Second, it has helped me to develop new products and services that have been successful in the market.

Third, it has helped me to create a culture of innovation that has allowed my company to stay ahead of the competition.

Maintaining a CEO mindset requires intentional daily habits and routines. I begin each day with a mindful morning ritual that includes exercise, goal setting, and visualizing success. This sets a positive tone for the day and aligns with my focus.

Regular check-ins with my leadership team foster clear communication and provide insights into various aspects of the business. Continually learning through reading, podcasts, or industry forums ensures I stay informed and adaptable. Finally, dedicating time to reflect on achievements, setbacks, and lessons learned helps me refine my approach and evolve as a leader.

I have implemented some habits and daily routines to help maintain and strengthen my CEO mindset:

Reading. I read books and articles about leadership, innovation, and business strategy. This helps me stay current on the latest trends and learn from other leaders' experiences.

Networking. I meet with other CEOs and entrepreneurs to learn from their experiences and share my own. This helps me stay connected to the business community and ahead of the curve. SAB (Strategic Advisor Board) is a perfect example of this. I network with all the team leaders and have learned so much from them. Sometimes, it is praise for a job well done; sometimes, it is constructive criticism. Networking with CEOs and entrepreneurs is essential. Through SAB, I even do a weekly video called "Been There/Done That" (https://www.youtube. com/playlist?list=PLfEf_UOFtYdtkEN801OWYGE2SWv_ ym6I0), where I share a three-to-five-minute video each week with my thoughts on trending topics. It's a way of giving back and sharing my thoughts and ideas with other entrepreneurs.

Reflection. I take time daily to reflect on my goals, progress, and challenges. This helps me focus on my vision and ensure I am on track to achieve my goals. Getting caught up in the hustle and bustle of our daily lives is too easy, and we forget that we must take the time to reflect to ensure we stay on track.

Prac*ticing mindfulness.* I practice mindfulness meditation every day. Not in the meditation sense, but I run (or walk at a fast pace) on the treadmill each morning, which is my de-stress and relaxing time. This helps me stay present and focus on the tasks of the day.

Take these suggestions into consideration:

Be curious and open-minded. The best leaders are constantly learning and growing. They always look for new ways to improve their businesses and stay ahead of the competition. I am a lifelong learner. The world is constantly changing and evolving; you will be left behind if you do not keep up.

Be willing to take risks. Innovation often requires taking risks. The best leaders are fearless in failing. They learn from their mistakes and keep moving forward. I am not afraid of risk. My whole fifteen-year skydiving journey started with my first jump, which was to face my fear of heights. As the old saying goes, "You never know until you try."

Be able to see the big picture. The best leaders can see the big picture and understand the long-term implications of their decisions. They are focused on more than short-term results. This is why networking, finding a mentor, and communication are essential. Sometimes, we need that outside source to help us see the big picture.

Be able to communicate your vision. The best leaders can communicate their vision to others and inspire them to share it. They can articulate their vision clearly, concisely, and inspiringly. Often, what we think others already know isn't quite the case. We must communicate. And no one knows what is going on in your mind unless you articulate that.

In case you don't believe me, look at Steve Jobs. In 1984, he presented at the annual shareholders meeting of Apple Computer. In this presentation, Jobs introduced the Macintosh computer, a revolutionary product that changed how people interacted with computers. At the time, most computers were command-line interfaces, which were difficult to use. On the other hand, the Macintosh had a graphical user interface (GUI), making it much easier for people to use.

In his presentation, Jobs described the Macintosh as "the computer for the rest of us." He also said the Macintosh would "change the world." At the time, many people thought that Jobs was crazy. They didn't know there was a market for a computer that was easy to use. However, Jobs was right. The Macintosh was a huge success, revolutionizing how people interacted with computers. His vision for the Macintosh was something no one else was thinking about at the time. He saw the potential of a computer that was easy to use, and he was able to communicate that vision to others. As a result, the Macintosh revolutionized the computer industry.

Here are other examples of people who communicated their visions and revolutionized something:

Henry Ford. Ford had a vision of a car that was affordable for everyone. He could communicate this vision to others and make his vision a reality. The Model T Ford was a huge success, making cars accessible.

Walt Disney. Disney had a vision of a theme park that was unlike anything that had ever been seen before. He could communicate this vision to others and make his dream a reality. Disneyland was a huge success and changed how people thought about theme parks.

Mahatma Gandhi. Gandhi had a vision of an India that was free from British rule. He communicated this vision to others and led India to independence. Gandhi's vision changed the course of history. This shows you how communicating your vision can pave the way to success for you or, at the very least, let your mentors or others offer their feedback for your direction.

In closing, the examples of visionary individuals like Henry Ford, Walt Disney, and Mahatma Gandhi highlight the transformative power of effectively communicating one's vision. These trailblazers envisioned a future different from the status quo and shared their dreams with others, igniting a movement that changed industries, perceptions, and even nations. Their stories testify to a well-communicated vision's profound impact on shaping the world around us.

As you embark on your journey toward visionary leadership and strategic thinking, remember that your ideas have the potential to reshape paradigms, inspire innovation, and drive progress. By harnessing the art of communication and sharing your vision with conviction and clarity, you can create a ripple effect that touches lives, sparks change, and propels you toward your own pinnacle of success.

So, whether you're shaping the future of a business, a community, or even a nation, embrace the lessons from these visionary pioneers. As you articulate your dreams, rally supporters, and bring your aspirations to life, you become a catalyst for transformation, forging a path toward a brighter and more purposeful tomorrow.

Your visionary mindset, coupled with the skill of effective communication, is your compass on this remarkable journey of leadership and impact.

ABOUT THE AUTHOR

Patricia Baronowski-Schneider stands at the pinnacle of a distinguished career spanning over 35 years in the domains of investor relations (IR), public relations (PR), media relations, and marketing. With a track record marked by excellence, she has consistently delivered award-winning results for both herself and her esteemed clients.

Patricia's journey commenced within prestigious firms such as Handy & Harman, Citigate Dewe Rogerson, and The Altman Group, where she acquired invaluable insights and expertise. In 2010, she embarked on an entrepreneurial venture that would reshape the industry. Patricia founded Pristine Advisers, an agency that has become synonymous with excellence in the fields of IR and PR.

As a published author, Patricia has shared her wealth of knowledge in influential books on investor relations, public relations, and business. Her contributions to the industry literature have solidified her position as a thought leader. Alongside her professional achievements, Patricia has been honored with numerous awards, affirming her commitment to advancing the field.

Actively engaged in her local business community, Patricia is a proud member of the Farmingdale Chamber of Commerce. Her dedication to fostering connections and collaborations within the industry has been widely recognized.

Patricia's impact extends far beyond her immediate circle; she has been featured in and on the pages of various magazines and newspapers. Her insights and expertise have garnered her respect and admiration from peers and colleagues alike.

At Pristine Advisers, Patricia leads a team that empowers companies worldwide to strategically position themselves in front of their most critical audiences. With a vast database and an expansive network comprising over 800,000 targeted contacts, Pristine Advisers specializes in precisely conveying its clients' missions and objectives to the right audience.

Patricia's core belief centers on consistency and the delivery of top-notch quality, principles that are woven into the fabric of Pristine Advisers' operations. She firmly asserts that these principles are the keystones to achieving exceptional outcomes, and they underpin every facet of her work.

In a dynamic industry where success hinges on dedication, expertise, and an unwavering commitment to excellence, Patricia Baronowski-Schneider is a true visionary. Her resolute leadership has shaped the trajectory of the investor relations and public relations landscape, unlocking new possibilities and charting a course toward unparalleled success. Go to pristineadvisers.com for more information.

STRATEGIES FOR CREATING AND EXECUTING A COMPELLING VISION

PATRICK LAING

As I think about the characteristics of a visionary CEO, three words come to mind. They all start with F. The first, of course, is faith. You have to believe that it's possible. No matter how grandiose, how outlandish—maybe even crazy—your vision might seem to others, you have to believe that it's doable. It's a fundamental principle, a foundation for everything in life and business. You have to be able to see it. It's right there in the word. Visionary CEOs have a vision of what they want to accomplish.

Along with that, you must be fearless. You must have the vision to get there and the fortitude—another F word—to keep going when the going gets rough. You will invariably run into challenges, struggles, hurdles, and obstacles. It's guaranteed. You'll fall on your face many times, in most cases, whenever you try to build something special. You must fail forward though. It's vital that you don't give up. Maybe the word fortitude is better than fearless, but fearless has to be part of it. You can't get thrown off just because the going gets hard. We all have a fear of missing out. We have a fear of the unknown, a fear of uncertainty. But visionary CEOs step out into the dark, having faith they'll land on their feet and knowing that whatever life throws at them, whatever their project places in their path, they can overcome it one way or another.

The third F is the word fellowship. I firmly believe that no CEO can accomplish great things without a great team around them, without fellowship and the support, encouragement and skill set of those "in the trenches" with them. They say that behind every successful man is a woman either scratching her head or cheering him on—usually, the latter (let's hope!). But the same principle applies: $1 + 1 = 3$. I've said for a long time that $1 + 1 = 11$ but that's only when they stand side-by-side. There's a multiplier. A visionary CEO must surround himself or herself with people they can trust and believe in. They must rely on mentors, coaches, other executives, and more. They can't do it alone. If they try, they'll either burn out or ostracize and alienate people who, if they had just delegated to, trusted, and believed in, would have been honored to be a part of their vision and help out in making it happen.

These are the three principles, or characteristics, that distinguish visionary CEOs. There are many more as well, but these three are fundamentally important. There's another F word for you. These are fundamental to the success of any CEO.

Just as with the last topic of "characteristics" of a visionary CEO, there are three key examples from my life that best illustrate this question … the question of what, from my experiences, has inspired me to seek to be just that.

The first was the opportunity I had to serve in the U.S. Army. In the military, you have a lot of resources, leadership, and pressure all around. But one of the great things about the military is that they are always looking ahead and preparing for worst-case scenarios. That's where our training goes. That's where our billions of dollars as taxpayers go—into preparing for the worst outcome possible—war. As a visionary CEO, we have to do the same. We have to prepare for the worst but build for the best, and believe that it can come to pass, but always be prepared for the hurdles, bumps, and bruises that come along the way. If we're surprised by the growing pains, we'll have more difficulty getting over and through them. Expect them and you'll do just fine.

One of my favorite quotes describes the level of our frustration being equal to "the distance between our expectations and reality." That doesn't mean we lower our standards, but we do lower our expectations, maybe of others around us, of how easy the road will be, of the growing pains that will happen, blips in the road, bottlenecks, challenges, and lessons that we're sure to undergo. The less we do this, the more frustrated and overwhelmed we will be. It as simple as that. The more we feel this way, the more it will impact our growth, our ability to lead, and our quality of life.

The second experience in my life was serving a full-time service mission for my church for two years in central Italy. I learned a lot from the Italians. They have many problems and challenges, but one thing they do is truly live life to its fullest. They suck the marrow out of life, as Robin Williams spoke of in the classic movie, The Dead Poets Society. They are passionate about food, wine, music, love, and family and make the most of every day it seemed.

There are many challenges in Italy. There are challenges with their economy. There's a lot of drug use. There's a lot of crime and corruption. They have their fair share of difficulties indeed. But, despite those difficulties, they live life with a compelling level of passion, energy, and love. They're world famous for it. They have some of the best food, arts, fashion, and sports in the world; the list goes on. They throw their hearts and souls into what they do. It's a great example of a visionary mindset, looking to the future and making the most of every moment, even if you're still determining how you'll get there. You may be tired, uncertain, and feel overwhelmed at times. A lot of the youth in Italy feel overwhelmed and discouraged, and yet, most of them don't give up. As mentioned, that is a key to being a visionary CEO.

I also learned a great deal from my parents who started a business when I was a young man. This would be the third experience I've had that impacted me and left an indelible impression. They franchised it all over the world. We made more money than we could imagine. But we also made mistakes. We learned that you must keep balance when you're building a business. You have to be careful. Otherwise, it can easily grow out of control. It can outgrow you and consume you if you're not aware.

It was a lesson, I suppose, of what not to do. We knew as a family that our business had the potential to keep growing and making a great deal of income, touching many lives. But we also came to see how it was impacting us, and not for the positive. We had to learn some tough lessons on how to maintain balance in our actions. I try to apply that today in my life and business. I work hard and put in long hours. I have a vision of where we can take this, but I do try to keep balance, work hard, play hard, and ensure the business isn't running us. One thing I do personally to help with this is I take a week off once a month and go somewhere nice. I may still do some work but it's on the beach, up in the mountains or, maybe, visiting my parents back home. I try to "step back" from the chaos of my normal schedule. It really seems to help out.

How does a CEO develop a compelling vision for their organization? How does this impact the overall company strategy?

First and foremost, the CEO or management team must be crystal clear about who they are and what they stand for. A vision has to be founded on principles. I'm referring to "eternal" principles or principles that don't change with every wind or whisper. They're rules that are unchangeable, like gravity. There are laws that dictate the outcome. There are principles that are "set in stone." And if your vision and organization are founded in such immutable laws, you're much more likely to get to and end up where you want to be.

Second, it does you no good to just keep it in your head. You must share your vision with your team. It's why mission statements and public goals are so important. They can be highlighted on the wall. Everyone can see them—employees, clients, the community, and more. How can anyone get behind your vision if they don't know what it is?

Third, you have to make sure that people understand it. Make sure it's clear and concise. Make sure it's compelling and that the people not only understand it but also believe in it (or at least in you). You have to drive it home. It has to be a part of who you are, of everything you do—what you say, what you talk about, how you live, and how you lead. An employee on their very first day should hear about what you stand for. An employee who's been there for years should know your "mission" or vision by heart. If you ever ask an employee, team member, or contractor what your vision or mission is, they should be able to recite it immediately by memory.

In addition, as the company or management team is developing this vision, you must also get feedback and input from your team. There are different perspectives on this, but I'm an open book. I have an open-door policy in our company, and it's served us very well. That doesn't mean we give the team all the decision-making power. That doesn't mean we relinquish control. But we do open our minds and ears to their ideas.

Two amazing things happen by being open to input and feedback from your team. Number one, you inevitably get some really great ideas. And two, you get far more buy-in from your team. That's the next essential principle when it comes to developing a compelling vision.

If you have a clear and concise vision—if it's public and not private, if it's repeated and reinforced on an ongoing basis, and if your employees buy in to it—you will have people who will stay forever. They feel appreciated. They feel excited and inspired. They feel like they have some say in their futures. They feel like they are contributing to the company itself and the direction it's moving. They feel like they have "ownership" in what you're creating. And, if your employees have an ownership mindset in what they do and take accountability for their work and treat it as though it was their personal company, you are a thousand times more likely to accomplish your goals and achieve your potential. As I said, this is a critical, fundamental, eternal (even) principle on which a company should be built. Any visionary CEO who has succeeded or hopes to succeed should has figured this out for themselves.

If you truly want to balance innovation and risk-taking with maintaining stability and sustainable growth in the organization, your people, staff, employees, and contractors must have this ownership mindset. They need to be encouraged, but also held accountable. This isn't something a CEO can do by him-or-herself. They must have the support and protection of a like-minded team.

I helped co-author a book on accountability with Adam Torres called Mission Matters in 2022 where I discussed the importance of not being a victim and not, as we call it, living "beneath the line." The most important question we can ask ourselves is illustrated in the classic book The Oz Principle, which refers to staying above or constantly "living above the line." The critical question we all need to ask ourselves is: What else can I do? Now, sometimes we need help. It's okay! Ask for it. It isn't being a victim to ask for a hand when we need it. We need to delegate and involve others in our work. If our entire team can assume this mindset and not point fingers, pass the buck, or say, "This isn't my job," but have an ownership mindset and take = accountability in this way, the entire organization will do better. It's much more likely to succeed even when it's taking risks.

It's important to take baby steps, line upon line, precept upon precept. Don't try to bite off more than you can chew. Don't jump so far into the deep end that you drown. It's crucial you take risks, have innovation, but also be wise. To that point, again—and this is a recurring theme—don't do it alone. I'm not just talking about your team. I'm not just talking about those you might involve or delegate to or ask for help or those who you are managing. I'm talking about those who are much wiser than you, more experienced, people who have trod the path ahead of you, maybe a mentor or a coach or an executive of a successful company you have a relationship with or someone else you look up to.

By turning to people like this for direction, you can avoid pitfalls. You'll learn shortcuts, overcome obstacles, shorten your learning curve and save time. If you do this, you're more likely to succeed without the same failure, pain, and heartache that so many CEOs have to endure as they're figuring it out. That's what all of us wish for our own kids, that they will do better than we did and that they won't make the same mistakes, that they will learn faster, go farther, and be able to accomplish more.

The same thing should apply to being a CEO. We all have a vision of where we want to go, but if we can learn from others who have already "been there and done that," we can avoid the same growing pains, regrets, and mistakes that so many of us, unfortunately, undergo. It's an important reminder. We should remember that we have two ears and one mouth. This applies to our team and being open to their feedback. It applies to mentors, coaches, and leaders. It can apply to our significant others, our partners, and friends. We must be open to input. We must be humble to be successful CEOs. So often, we're not. We know too much. We know where we're going. We know what we want to do. And come hell or high water, we're going to get there. We'll do better if we can remember to listen and be open to input more.

If we take accountability and admit when we fall short our people will give us the shirts off their backs. They'll turn to us and look to us as true leaders, people whom they want to follow, protect, support, and emulate. This is the essence of being a visionary CEO because we're looking both forward and outward, behind, left, right, up, and down. We're looking at what we're doing and how it will impact our people—not just our company but our future and maybe even our community and nation as a whole. Those are principles that successful visionary CEOs seek to recall.

I worked for a remodeling firm in Portland, Oregon named Lifeguard Northwest for several years. I had an extraordinary general manager I worked with named Roy Bletko. I learned a great deal from Roy, probably more than any employer or supervisor I've met in over thirty-five years in business and sales.

As the sales director for the company, I had a great deal of autonomy. It's one of the things that Roy did well; he rarely micromanaged us. He hired good people. He taught us what we needed to do our job. But he let us make it our own. I've talked in this chapter about the importance of creating ownership in our people. Roy was a master at this, I came to see. With his leadership, our management team taught our teams two principles that made an enormous difference in our success. One of those is the book I mentioned earlier, The Oz Principle. It teaches accountability. It teaches you to keep asking, "What else can I do? Am I approaching this problem with a victim mindset by pointing fingers, passing the buck, and saying 'this isn't my job' or 'I don't know where to start.'" The book refers to that as "living below the line." It says that if you can learn to live above the line, as they call it, and keep asking the question, "What else can I do?" then amazing things will happen. It's true. I saw it on a daily basis at LeafGuard.

The challenge lies in the initial step or challenge you encounter, followed by the subsequent step you must take to address it. Now, that doesn't mean you have to do it alone. It's not weak to ask for help, as mentioned previously. On the contrary, it's empowering to say, "Let's do this together," and to delegate well. Do so and you show your people you trust them and have faith in them. They may not do it exactly as you would have, but don't burden yourself by trying to do it all on your own. You'll enjoy more balance, time freedom, and respect from your team. You'll empower them, in fact. You'll build faith and trust in them as well. You'll build long lasting relationships, and invariably, get more done. You'll also grow your people in ways you simply couldn't without delegating.

At LeafGuard Northwest, we were a subsidiary of Beldon Home Solutions out of San Antonio, Texas. We were one of sixty-five offices nationwide. By applying these principles in our work we quickly became the # 1 branch in the country, out of 65 offices nationwide. We often sold more than # 2 Chicago and # 3 Seattle combined. How did we do that? The Oz Principle and accountability empowerment principles it teaches were the first key. The second was a lesson in execution Roy shared with us.

Roy is a great example of a visionary leader. He inspired and empowered us. He didn't micromanage us but gave us principles to build upon to take the company to the next level, to help fulfill his vision. And we did exactly that. We grew from $3.5 million in 2000 to $7.5 million in 2010, $16 million in 2011, and $20 million in annual sales revenue in 2020. Eventually, I was promoted to national sales trainer and traveled nationwide, teaching other offices how to do what we had done. The second principle we taught our team that contributed to this is from Stephen Covey, the world-renowned author of The Seven Habits for Highly Effective People. It's a methodology called the Four Disciplines of Execution and it changed our whole company as we knew it. I encourage you to look it up; you can easily find it on YouTube.

The Four Disciplines teach that you should have what they refer to as a "Wildly Important Goal" or in other words a "WIG." You should have "Lag Measurements" that measure whether you are achieving your goal or are on track to achieve it. Then you have to "Lead Activities" like you would if trying to lose weight. Your goal isn't focused on calories consumed when trying to lose weight; you're focused on how many pounds you lose. But that's not what helps you lose weight. You must measure calories. You must measure time spent at the gym. You must measure and keep score so you know if you're winning or not. There's a lot more that goes into it. But these are two things we taught and two lessons I learned and have applied several times since. They worked and were life-changing for our company, team, and me.

To cultivate a growth mindset and foster a culture of continuous learning, you must lead by example. There are too many managers and executives who lead from behind a desk. They're never in the field. They're rarely if ever hands-on. As a sales director, I used to do ride-alongs at least once a week to get out with my team. "Let's run a couple of appointments together" was my favorite message. "You watch me do one, and I'll watch you do one." Usually, I'd watch them first because I didn't want them to get any ideas. They had already been trained. They knew what they were supposed to do, but I wanted to see how well they were doing it.

Then we'd maybe take a break for lunch and talk about the first attempt. I'd share with them my notes, give them some feedback, and then we'd run another appointment. This time I would model how it should be done. Learning is not just book learning. It's learning on the job. It's learning hands-on. It's learning by doing more than anything else, in my opinion. But we as leaders must be willing to get in the trenches and model appropriate behavior, actions, correct principles, and skills. We must model these things ourselves. We must create opportunities for our team to learn via seminars, workshops, continuing education, and more. Make sure it's available, funded, affordable, and fun. It's something they should look forward to.

Lastly, I'm a big believer in recognition and reward. When somebody is stepping up and going the extra mile—getting certified, additional training and licensing, or whatever the case might be—whether they're doing it on their own or as part of a company-funded program, it's important that we recognize and reward them for it with bonuses, SPIFs, paid time off, and the like. These are important. Not everybody is motivated simply by learning. Not all reps are motivated by income. It's different for each one. But amazing things can happen if we try to make it fun, recognize them for their efforts, and reward them, even if it's just verbally in front of the group.

Employees respond well to seeing a leader, an executive, model how to do things then ask what could have been done better. We're not just telling them what to do; we're showing them how to do it. We're not just managing from the back room, from the penthouse suite. We're out there showing them how to do it. Obviously, there are limitations to that, especially with the size of an organization, but there needs to be management that's managing—and not only managing but also modeling. It's imperative to our work.

We need to give them opportunities to grow, learn, and be challenged. There are ways to gamify learning these days, such as creating contests, interactive activities, and more. When I worked for Sears years ago, I sold refrigerators and freezers, and they had a whole series of continuing education modules that we could do on our own time. Every time you finished one, or a section of these modules, you received a button or a ribbon. But people were serious about earning those awards. It was a badge of honor. It was something they were proud of.

We learned a lot in the process, about ourselves and also our team. We made it into something that was looked highly on and could even result in pay raises, extra bonuses, and more. Everyone really got into it. We were young, hungry salespeople, but that added incentive to learn and grow and become all that we could be was a powerful motivator. I've always tried to remember that. I think most of us could do a better job of it in our lives and careers. Do it well and incredible things happen. The team typically responds well and, together, we invariably accomplish more.

Several things can help us manage stress and maintain mental well-being. I'm a big believer that so much of it comes down to our thoughts and our mindset. We must stay optimistic, focus on that vision, and "keep our eye on the prize." The direction we're heading can easily become cloudy or unclear. It's easy to feel weighed down by the challenges of building a business. How we view the journey, the challenges, and the potential benefits and blessings (i.e., our vision) impacts us, those we work with, the direction we're moving, and ultimately our success. How do we truly view where we are, how we're getting there, how our team is doing along the way, and more?

As visionary CEOs, we must be eternal optimists and realists, but we must be focused and driven enough and able to keep our eye on the prize—with our proverbial glass half-full versus half-empty, as they say. I know this from experience. I've learned this in classes and from my own successes and failures. I've seen throughout my career that we can choose how we feel, and what we do with those feelings and thoughts. After all, what dictates how we feel are inherently the thoughts that we tell ourselves.

A good example is when two employees were sent home from work. There was a virus going around, and they both had it. They were told, "You're contagious. You need to go home and be off for two weeks before you come back. Don't worry, we'll pay you for your time. You just can't be here. We're trying to stop the spread," and they were both sent home.

One of the employees said to himself, "I can't afford to be off work for two weeks. My inbox is already full; it's overflowing! I'm already behind on several of my projects. I've got people waiting on me to do my part. I can't believe this." He went home and was miserable for the next two weeks.

The second employee, who had the same workload, the same overflowing inbox, emails coming out of his ears, deadlines, demands, and so forth said, "Awesome! I've needed a vacation. They're going to pay me?! Are you kidding. This is great! They didn't say I couldn't go fishing." He went home, rented some movies, bought a bunch of junk food, went fishing and hiking and spent time with his dog. He really enjoyed his two-week "break."

So, what was the difference between these two employees? The only difference is how they chose to view the situation. They both came back to the same overflowing inboxes, demands, and deadlines, but one came back depleted, frustrated, and stressed. The other came back invigorated and refreshed, even excited. There's an important lesson to be learned in this example.

How do we improve our mindsets? There are lots of ways, of course. Having written goals that you review daily usually helps. Reading motivational books and listening to uplifting music. Good health and fitness can most definitely contribute. Personally, I try to go swimming every morning and sit in the hot tub for a few minutes. This gets me a little exercise and a little sunshine as well. This might sound a little bit funny, but it's been said that if you stand barefoot on the grass, away from a street, any pollutants, or toxins, the energy from the earth will do amazing things for how you feel and your outlook for the day. I don't know how true this is, but as I walk out to the pool, I do try to walk on the grass. I also try to get enough sleep. It's been said that if you sleep in ninety-minute blocks, you'll sleep more deeply and wake up more refreshed, which impacts your mental well-being and what you can ultimately accomplish. It has to do with your circadian rhythms. It's better to get seven and a half hours of sleep than eight, for example, because if you sleep that extra thirty minutes, you're cutting into another ninety-minute window, and you won't feel as refreshed when you wake up. You won't be as aligned or ready as you would have been. Sleeping six hours is actually better than seven because it's precisely four ninety-minute blocks. Try it out if you'd like. It really works.

In our company, our sales team spans across the country. We have associates from coast to coast and clients in all fifty states. So, we're a remote work organization. We don't see people in person. We're usually meeting over Zoom. We did do a big company get together here in Las Vegas last year. We met people with whom we felt a kinship and friendship but had never met face-to-face. It was a surreal experience.

One of the ways we foster curiosity, camaraderie, loyalty, and vision within our team is to try to meet at least twice a week over Zoom. As I said, we're spread across the country so this is how we have to do it, but it works great. We do a little bit of housekeeping, a little bit of training. We recognize those who are performing. We open up to Q&A and just try to connect as a team. Most of all we try to, on an ongoing basis, paint the picture, the "vision," as it were, of who we are, where we're going, and how we want to get there. It's an ongoing challenge to continue to groom the team's collective mindset. Connecting with them in this way—where they're interacting at least once, if not twice, a week—has been a key piece of it in our minds.

I talk a lot about our open-door policy and how we truly want their feedback and input, and that's also a big piece of it all. We'll talk about a new product line we're looking at bringing on, or we'll talk about a challenge we're facing. We'll talk about a direction we want to head, an achievement we're trying to accomplish, or maybe the challenges we're running into getting there as a team. They feel like they have a voice. It contributes a great deal to our success. I like to announce things that are coming and dangle a carrot of sorts to pique their curiosity, I guess you could say. I often tell people that I have a "big announcement coming up next Tuesday that I'm excited about. Have a great weekend. Make sure you don't miss the meeting on Tuesday because you won't want to miss this." They come, expectant, and engaged.

This is just one way we foster a sense of curiosity and creativity. We encourage them to look for product lines that we could represent. We encourage them to introduce guests who could be on our radio show. I'm a headliner host on VoiceAmerica, a weekly radio show named Finding Certainty (find it at www.certaintylive.com if you'd like). It's a talk show where I interview guests from all over the world, focused on the topic of Certainty. I encourage my team members to look for good guests who would make worthy interviewees on my show. And, do you know what? They do.

Involving our team in these type of collaborative, creative, and mutually inspiring efforts has produced great results for us and our company. Another thing we've started doing as a company is that we realized we could do more than just make an income, we could also make a difference as a team. This was a collective effort and idea. It was a combined conversation and "discovery," as it were, that we all wanted to do more than just do business. We wanted to do good as a team. As a result, we collectively designed, built, formulated, and developed a program we now call the Certainty Partners Program. Through this we help nonprofits raise unlimited, zero-cost funding. We do this in several ways, but in the process, we're making an impact not just a buck. It's about more than our ledger, but our legacy, we like to say.

We also recently started formulating what we're calling the Certainty Fellowship a program designed to help college students afford college and even graduate 100% debt-free. This is an internship program through which they gain skills, insights, and mentorship. They gain access, make connections, and can even earn income that can enable them to pay for their schooling so they don't graduate encumbered with a bunch of student debt. We aim for them to graduate 100% debt-free, with money in the bank. So, involving our team in ideas and approaches like this that can make a difference is another way we foster creativity, innovation, excitement, loyalty, performance, results, and so much more in the process. It's been an honor to be a part of it. We're just getting better every day.

I'm asked at times what habits or routines do I do to maintain and strengthen my "Visionary CEO" mindset? First, I try to elicit feedback and input from those around me—mentors, partners, coaches, team members, and my wife, Tessha, of course. I'm a big believer in sounding boards. I don't know all things. I am not a jack of all trades. I have my own insights and experience from thirty-eight years in business. But there's a lot more I don't know than there is that I do. So, receiving feedback from people who care and even those who are further removed from me is valuable.

I was a member of Vistage Worldwide for a long time, so I'd meet once a month with a group of CEOs who did not have a vested interest in my business or me, but they did care about my success. We became friends. We had strong relationships, but we could give honest, even harsh, feedback when someone needed it. These were incredible CEOs, so they don't often need a kick in the butt. But, having that honest, accountable, professional input from unbiased parties is, really, worth its weight in gold.

In addition to this, I read a lot. I read fiction, nonfiction, historical biographies, and the scriptures as well. I learn a lot from the examples of good and bad leaders who have left us examples from which we can learn. I try to get on my knees and pray about the day. I've learned as a husband, father, church leader, and business leader that, when we try to do it on our own, we rarely do as well as we could with a little help. And, that includes help from above. Whatever you believe, whether it's God, the Universe, Allah, or just plain old inspiration, it's essential that we learn to listen and learn.

In my experience, I receive quite a bit of input, direction, impressions, and promptings, mostly because I expect them to flow into my life. I might have an idea come to me that I need to call someone, and when I ignore it, I find out later that I shouldn't have. When I listen, pick up the phone, and make that call, many times, it's exactly what I needed to do right then. The more I personally listen to these promptings and impressions, the better I do and the more impact I am able to have.

One of the most important daily routines (or daily habits) I've tried to implement in my life—and I've said this throughout this chapter—is listening to people around me and also to that higher power. I've found that He truly cares about us. He cares about what we're doing and is a lot closer to us than many of us realize. If we try to listen and learn, that vision we're seeking to accomplish becomes ever clearer. It becomes much more likely that we will achieve it and much less likely that we'll stumble and fall and make the mistakes that so many do, especially if we're learning from others who have already been down the path ahead of us, which shortens our learning curve and helps us avoid pitfalls along the way. When we listen, stay humble, and stay teachable most of all, we keep an open mind and do better in the short and long term.

I used to set a lot of New Year's resolutions, and about five or six years ago, I started setting one main resolution each year: to listen to every impression. When an idea comes to us, more often than not, I believe it's coming from somewhere important. It's coming from above. It's something that we should pay heed to. Not always. Sometimes, it's our own idea. Other times it's indigestion. But the more we listen the better we'll get at deciphering these promptings and using them in our life. We have to weigh the pros and cons and listen to how we feel. If we feel peaceful and calm, that's usually a good sign that we are on the right path.

I probably sound like a broken record, but if you are an aspiring leader looking to develop your visionary mindset, strategic thinking, and leadership capabilities, you need to remember you have two ears and one mouth. Surround yourself by people who will raise you up, not tear you down, but also people who will be honest in their feedback and support. They say we are the sum total of the five people we spend the most time with. I believe it. I firmly support spending time with people who raise us to a higher standard, whether that's mentors, colleagues, friends, or even family. Make sure you're spending time with people you aspire to be like and who help hold you to that higher standard and raise you to higher levels. Try to do the same for others. It comes back full circle. It's reciprocal, serendipitous, and real.

In addition to this, we should learn from those around us and those who went before us. I read a lot like I said. I like biographies. I enjoy examples from the classics like Plato and Dante, from leaders like Benjamin Franklin and George Washington, to more contemporary leaders like Malcolm Gladwell and Simon Sinek. There's a lot of expertise out there and a lot of experience. It's a waste not to try to learn from them.

If you're not a reader, listen to a book on Audible or a podcast channel as you work out or commute to and from work. Seek knowledge. Not only will it help you shorten your own learning curve, but you'll become a better person, and leader, in the process. You'll become a richer, deeper, multilayered leader, which is exactly the kind of leader with integrity that companies need—yes, that our very nation needs.

Another suggestion is to proactively seek opportunities to meet people, develop relationships, and get to know others in your industry throughout your career. Be proactive about it. Maybe you do it through networking or joining mindset groups or masterminds. I became a radio show host to expand my own circle of influence, and it worked. I have learned a great deal from interviewing accomplished celebrities, entrepreneurs, athletes, and more. It's been a really rewarding experience.

Whether you start a podcast, become a radio show host or a TV personality, you begin to speak or write, join masterminds and mentorship groups like Vistage, I recommend it. Not only will you learn a great deal and become more of who you can be, but you will also develop some great relationships too. You'll network with folks who may be able to help you in your business, and vice versa. You might become lifelong friends.

In conclusion, I do believe it's essential that you learn from and surround yourself by people who can help raise and inspire you to higher levels. Learn from the classics, from experts, and other leaders. Watch videos on YouTube. Take classes, go to seminars and workshops when you can. Befriend people who are smarter than you and then proactively seek ways to expand your own vision, and mind. It's important. If you can do those things, you can truly become a much better Visionary CEO. You'll lead your people in new directions, accomplish much more, gain more satisfaction, and make a difference as you go. Your own vision will be realized. I wish you Godspeed..

Cultivating a
Visionary Mindset

Tony D'Urso

Being a visionary means that you are into planning the future with some imagination and wisdom. Nothing happens without a vision and a plan, and not focusing on the future means the future really doesn't happen. Or, better put, the future doesn't happen the way you would best like to see it happen.

When I work "in" the business with a focus on getting things done, I find that the company's future does not fare as well as it should. Working in the business, while effective, is better reserved for a COO who can focus on the important tasks that have to be done throughout all the departments of the organization. While a CEO in a smaller organization has to act as the COO to get things done, he will find that he must focus on the future for some part of his day or week for the future survival of his company.

One key characteristic to this is literally the vision, at the top. Where is the company supposed to go in the next year? What accomplishments are really needed? What must be done, for the company to grow in market share, or even survive at all in the next year?

Another key characteristic is why. Why does the business need to be at a certain level in the next year? Or better put, what is the purpose of the company that acts as the fuel for the company to excel in its plans? Without the characteristic of a strong purpose, any company will naturally not do as well as it should. A strong purpose keeps things going. A weak purpose does not.

The characteristic of strategy is most likely the key that distinguishes a visionary CEO from a traditional one. It is effective strategies in place that have companies take over market share and create altogether new markets and dominate them. Simply working the company's business, on a day to day, and week to week basis will eventually see the demise of that company because the world changes. Nothing stays the same. One has to look far into the future and figure the best moves to maneuver into the best projected spots. And as CEOs know, even the best vision and strategies in place do not equate to success.

Keeping track of the pulse of the future is another key characteristic for the reasons just given. If everything stayed the same, then this would be an altogether different ballgame, but it does not. While you can be good at some things, and not at other things, i.e. superpowers, it is a matter of recognizing what you are best at, and how you can use that to create, mold, and drive your company into the future. Depending on your industry, there may be other characteristics that you need to adopt, but those mentioned are key and pivotal to the growth of any business.

A fast summation of the points just stated as some of the key characteristics are:

- A clear-cut vision of where the company should be a year or two from now

- A strong purpose that can propel the company into that future
- Well-defined strategies of how to obtain and/or create market shares
- Determination of what you are best at (superpowers) and understanding of how they can be used to create, mold, and drive your company into the future

The pivotal moment that inspired me to adopt a visionary mindset was during a seven-year period having four major federal or governmental protocols or rules that forced a re-write of the business plan and business mindset. It was the constant mandates that made me realize how we as a company, needed to better proof ourselves against any disastrous storms that we did not create and which we had no control over.

Only by the earlier mentioned characteristics was I able to put a thumbtack as a marker of where the business should be at in the future, that would help us navigate through any treacherous terrain no matter who put it there. This operational mindset influenced me to rethink my leadership, strategy, and organizational growth to a large degree. I took giant strides in a newly created market that I did not know well and did not understand sufficiently.

However, I was strong on my vision, my purpose, and the other characteristics earlier mentioned. I also recognized my superpowers and developed methodologies to fully take advantage of them. I developed a new market and took off. Meanwhile, the core business that was befuddled by constant rules and protocols, continued up and down like a cork in the ocean. Because of this, any business from that section was always considered as a boon, while the new market endeavors became the new business mode.

The leadership became fast. If something was not working or bringing in sufficient revenue, it caused a re-write or a re-think of our strategy, which then fueled growth. Too many mistakes were made. Issues beyond our control entered. Yet, we strove to grow, and it was the purpose coupled with a clear-cut vision that pulled us through. You have to be able to compare your actions against revenue coming in. And your purpose has to be there watching.

For example, you may be answering social media messages. That's nice. It may make you feel good, but is it bringing in revenue for the company? Is it helping you become the leader in your zone? Is it creating much goodwill for your company? What is it doing? Is it really needed? What is the purpose for answering 100s or even 1000s of messages? Are they related to your company's products and services? Or are they meaningless distractions which do not matter if they were ever answered?

When you look at something that way, it helps direct you to the best optimum action to take. Again, you have to keep revenue, your company's growth, its vision, and purpose in mind. These characteristics have to be there in whatever you do, whatever actions you take on your company's behalf. Doing so yields the fastest growth.

The best way to develop a compelling vision for your organization is to dream of what your company's future should be. This is a literal exercise and not to be taken for granted. The way to do this is with a pen and paper, and nothing else. No distractions. No music. No TV. No radio. Nothing that will distract you. Jordan Adler did this by going out to the park and spending the afternoon writing out his future as he describes in his bestselling book, *Beach Money*.

The way this works is to start dreaming of what you see yourself doing in the future. Pretend like you did when you were a child. Go into the future and look back at yourself and write down what you see as being accomplished. Decide on what you should be doing next year. Where are you at? What is the company doing? How big is it? What services or products has it developed? What is it selling?

As you can see by this, there are many, many questions to work out. This is why it will take you an afternoon to work this out. Do not consider this foolish or unproductive. It is these exact and precise steps that took me from an industry replete with constant mandates that changed my business, to the start of something brand new that I knew nothing about. I did work out my vision, purpose, long-term objective, master plan, and strategy of where I should take my business. Where am I going? What am I doing? How am I doing it?

Note that I did not say anything about finances or capital. There is none in this dream. This dream is simply that childish movie that you make of your future. Keep things within reason, of course, because you are not going to be the ruler of the world next year (and really, who would want that headache?). This dream is play-acting at its best because you make yourself imagine all sorts of products and services for your company, and no money was spent in its production. That's always fun, isn't it?

The exercise by itself is invigorating. It brings fresh gas to the engine of your company. It gives you that adrenaline that you needed. It's like planning a vacation. The future of your company is the vacation. Driving to the location is what you are doing, and the dream is your map. The more you dream, the more that you put into your dream, the more detailed your "vacation" becomes, and the more real that vision actually manifests.

I say this from experience and from teaching others how to do this. I know this can go over people's heads. I get that. That's why it takes study and practice. That's why you are studying this right now. Work on it. Ponder it. Relish it, and you will get somewhere. If you merely read this, and then go pick up a snack and watch something on your computer, then all of this knowledge and wisdom dissipates in the sky and is gone. Don't let this moment escape you. I made more than I ever did as a corporate boss. Yes, really. Once you learn how to create your own future, everything changes.

As a visionary CEO, you have no choice at times but to make the best decision that you can with the resources that you have at hand. No doubt you, as I have, may find that you spent too much capital or made too many mistakes in trying to balance innovation. I started in a brand-new industry to keep my company afloat because the existing business was riddled with government interference. That could not be changed without starting my own country. Thus, I had to innovate and work at something completely new. And in this case, it was also something that I knew nothing about, and had no experience in. Talk about zero-zero-zero in all respects.

What was it that propelled this new venture to grow beyond expectations? It was the thorough creation of a future by simply using the power of imagination (a.k.a. guided imagery and visualization) of what we would do, as a company, in the next year. It was as simple as that. Yet, make no mistake: the creation of that dream took weeks to mold and set up, and it required constant vigilance to keep it in place. That said, it worked tremendously.

Once you can see the success, in the future, that you are directing with your imagination, you then become more accustomed to that success. It becomes more familiar. It becomes expected. Therefore, when you are innovating and taking a risk at the same time, you will find that success and growth will far more likely appear because you have already directed yourself to seeing it occur in the future.

Once you can imagine that it actually can and will happen, then you can go forward in the real world, with the actions necessary to its accomplishment. Your confidence comes up that it will be successful. This confidence resonates through to the employees much like a tuning fork triggers another one. Those actions beget company stability. If the employees, and this includes subs and associates that do work for the company, are confident of the results, then it becomes unstoppable as they will take suitable actions to push through. Thus, if the employees and executives of the company are confident, this lends to a much greater success of the risk-taking from the top.

It is actions such as these that many companies grow and survive through changing times. Companies that do not balance innovation and risk-taking are more likely to fall by the wayside. Sit back and think about companies that have disappeared off the face of the earth. Even some of the most well-known and famous icons have drifted away to oblivion. The companies that are gone today are countless. What happened? You'll find their executives did not innovate and take the necessary risks to move with industry changes.

In 2007, I was at the helm of a lead-generation organization, and we brought in clients with a large appetite for leads. While the revenue was in the seven-digits, the lead generation industry was beset with regulations, mandates, and protocols that severely impacted the industry. Thus, at four different times, the company was brought down to its knees with the issuance of another federal or industry rule or standard. Four times in seven years was severe enough to consider looking for something that would not be at the mercy of such sweeping decisions.

When podcasting was looked into, it was decided that it could be a great asset to the company, to grow and develop in a new industry, while making needed adjustments in lead generation. However, this was a brand-new field to delve into. There was no existing audience. There was no radio/podcasting experience. People of extraordinary success (which we coined as "Elite Entrepreneurs" at the time) were not known. I worked on the future of what I saw myself doing in the company and where would I lead us into the next year.

As if I was making a movie, I saw myself podcasting, interviewing millionaires and billionaires who share their stories, advice, and wisdom to my audience. I saw a growing audience swell to the millions. I saw my podcast on all the major platforms out there—even platforms that I didn't know existed at the time. I saw myself with courses, with books, and making tremendous publicity. This could be frightening for anyone starting out on a new venture with absolutely no experience in it whatsoever. I worked at my vision and literally created it and wrote it down.

I then worked out the supporting steps to make that vision a reality. I worked out what my purpose was and my reason for doing it. I worked out an objective to attain in one to two years. I worked out a master plan that included strategy and tactical steps to achieve. I worked out the daily things to do that would vertically accomplish my vision. I set these in motion and in months I was generating over 10,000 downloads a month. Then that was weekly. And the numbers grew.

By my second year, my downloads were at 50,000 per episode and so on. Today, the people listening to my show are over 200,000 per episode. Many months I've had over a million people. Thus, I speak from complete experience on the key points to focus on that demonstrate the impact of visionary leadership that brings about great success.

The CEO sets the stage. The CEO lays out the bar, the hurdle, that the company needs to jump over to make its goals. The way to do this successfully in the organizations that I've operated and managed are to regularly discuss the overall vision and the objective of the company, and why those are important.

Left to its own devices, company employees are well-known to establish their own goals and objectives, which usually are not the topmost critical actions to the company. They mean well, but they are often subjected to industry talk and the shiny object syndrome. In other words, the employees are easily swayed by what is going on in the industry and are prone to make decisions and choices that are one-off and not necessarily based on a significant industry trend.

It does work both ways, and one must be careful to not miss out on a new trend. That said, when the company's vision and objectives are regularly in the limelight with the company at meetings, in announcements, in their newsletter, and whatever methods of communication they may have with the employees, it is also important to list out these items for key focus.

Focusing on the vision and objectives helps corral the attention and effort to what is really needed: the accomplishment of the company's goals. This is the most sure-fire approach to cultivating a growth mindset and fostering a culture of learning and improvement within the organization. As of result of this constant attention to the vision and objective, you will find less resistance and more acceptance in employee training.

Methods need to be in place on a regular basis to train employees to do their job more efficiently, as well as grow with the times. If employees do not keep on track with training, you can find in a short space of time, that the industry has completely changed, making the skill sets of existing employees not as valuable as they once were at the start. This is a major reason to continue the push of where you are taking the company, and the training becomes the train (pun intended) to take the employees to destination (accomplishment of the company's objectives).

There are three main activities to teach to manage stress and improve your mental well-being as an entrepreneur. First, when I have success at my endeavors and revenue comes in, I find myself at a low level of stress routinely. Reversely I find that when revenue is low or does not come in, that this creates a greater amount of stress. This is where burnout can come from if the stress carries on for too long. My remedy for this is to review my income machines and methods and ensure that everything is in place. You can work forever on just this past sentence as it is so broad.

Yet, it is this step that is so key for maintaining well-being as an entrepreneur. Recently I looked at my income machines and in a new unit, I decided I did not have enough income items. I saw that I needed more products and services to offer to my consumers. I created more and made those known to my public. That improved my stress level quickly. But then I found that it was perhaps too automated and needed a little more of a personal touch, so I adjusted how that was communicated to my public.

Second, another item, and perhaps more important is to change your focus. You will find that burnout occurs when you are focused on one thing for too long. As an entrepreneur, you are the key person in your company to get things done and there are usually a great number of items and distractions vying for your attention.

After a while, you may find increase in stress and burnout. The best thing to do is go out and work on your yard, go exercise, talk a walk, take a hike. Do something that takes you out of the office and looking around the world. When I had my last dog, I walked him several times a day. That was great to take my mind off work, even if I did not want to. I was forced. That was excellent and always kept me excited to jump back into work and get things done.

You must force yourself, if needed, and develop the routine to get out each and every single day, and walk your body while looking at the world you live in. I cannot stress enough how to beat stress by going out in the world and moving your own body for a short while.

The third point is probably the biggest for everyone in this day and time. This point is about how to handle distractions. The distractions are mind boggling and they come from everywhere. Online, in the world, in your office, everywhere. When I run around taking care of whatever comes in front of my eyes, I will find that I get tired more easily and that I need to change my focus as per an earlier step. This is a matter of self-discipline here because you must force yourself to stay on point.

No matter what happens, you must force yourself to finish the tasks that you started. You must force yourself to follow through on the steps that you laid out for yourself and your company that must get done. If you need any superpower, then this is the best one to have: the superpower of not being distracted. If you are never distracted, then (except for point one earlier mentioned) you will find you never get burnout. It is easier said than done, but it works and is necessary to keep your company growing. In my years of podcasting, every problem led back to one of these steps. Every time.

Your company grows through the purchases or sales of products or services. While there can be other factors, such as buying an apartment building and getting renters, it still comes down to the proper buying and selling of products or services. You should know what is popular and sells in your industry. You are probably checking the news feeds on a regular basis, and you should.

Sometimes, however, you have to look at new areas that have not been approached and thus develop new products and services. I did this when I went from lead generation as the main business to podcasting as the main business, with lead generation as the secondary income source. I built a big podcast out of sheer innovation to be able to control our revenue in an industry that was beset with rules and regulations at the drop of a hat.

It takes soul-searching, and it takes looking at the world and finding what you can control and what can you change. I found that I could do that with podcasting as it is not a heavily regulated industry. In fact, over time, all that became regulated were how downloads were calculated and verified. That was easy as the major podcast platforms put those regiments in place. I did not have to worry about that.

As a result, I was able to use social media for the purpose it was designed, and I promoted my weekly shows to an ever-growing audience. It was curiosity that started it for me. After the fourth protocol came down, I looked around and became curious about this world "podcast" that I kept hearing about. I looked into it and found that it was hardly regulated and gave the owner a lot of control. In fact, you could podcast from anywhere in the world.

When you find something that is not well regulated, you obviously find that you have freer rein and control. This means more income and it also means having more fun. I have tremendous fun podcasting. I do not discuss anything controversial, and I stay away from possible dangerous issues.

I tried to help business owners and entrepreneurs deal with the 2020 and 2021 worldwide issues at the time, but that was so regulated. I only received flak on a few episodes. Otherwise, I stayed away from the entire topic.

The mindset that there is an area of income that you can control is the start of your curiosity. When I first heard about podcasting, I did not have it fully tied into income. However, I knew that I could speak on a myriad of topics that were not censored. From there I knew I could develop income sources, and I did.

The most important habit and daily routine I have is that of answering my email as the first thing I do every day. I know others may do this last, but I do it first. I have clients out there. I have prospects out there. I have people that want to be on my show. I like to address those emails and any issues first thing in the day and get that out of the way.

It is a good feeling to have my plate relatively clean as first thing each day. I can address anything important to my employees, as needed, in addressing any situations. Then I can more freely work on my business instead of "in" my business. This frees my attention. Otherwise, I could have that nagging feeling and wonder if there is anything I should know about? I like to have a free conscience and answering all emails first thing clears them out of the way.

Another routine and habit I have is that of having a lunch break every day. While it can be only 5 minutes sometimes, at least I can fuel up and get back to work. My body works best when it has the nutrition it needs. Yes, I can skip a meal now and then. And yes, I can have a soda and chips now and then, if I really feel I must, but my body needs proper fuel to work at maximum. You're not putting mud in your car engine are you?

I also take that lunch time break to walk around, speak to someone else in person, and breathe some fresh air (if that's possible). This invigorates me to go another few hours in the afternoon. I work on my social media, the same as I do with my daily emails. There may be prospects asking questions, or clients, or fans of my company's products and services. I address all social media every day and I appreciate hearing from fans, as I'm sure they appreciate hearing from me.

As part of that, while there can be seemingly 100s or even 1000s of social media platforms, I stick to a few of the key platforms and make my presence known there. Even if you are only on two platforms, be there religiously and make it known where you hang out. While it may be nice to be on 100s of social platforms, you probably cannot be on them every day without hiring someone to answer your messages.

That is where I differ as I found out a long time ago that no one can answer my messages better than I can. I know my business better than anyone else so why should I pay someone to answer messages for me? I have never had it successfully work for me, and I used to be constantly embarrassed at the poor responses from someone hired to answer my messages. That taught me to do that part myself.

The result of all of this is that I know where everything stands and what my prospects, clients and sponsors may need from me. Then it becomes easier to order or engage in the necessary tasks to satisfy requirements.

As with lunch, so it is with dinner. I take that break, stretch my legs, speak to real people in front of me, go for a walk, and enjoy life. You can have different routines. Mine have served me for decades whether I was in corporate America, or a solo entrepreneur. I end the day with a clean slate, a clear mind, and a good feeling that I did my best.

Get the wisdom from Jordan Adler in *Beach Money*. Learn how to write down the vision for your enterprise. It may take you all day. My students usually take a few weeks to get a fully clear vision written out, even though it's only one very well-crafted sentence. Once that is done, flesh out the rest of the steps, which Jordan does not list, but which are innate and inherent in the entire process. Namely work out the purpose and get your "why" put down in writing, just underneath the vision.

After that, work out your objective. If you could have your dream come true by next year, what would that look like for your company? Be completely real and write down what can occur between now and then for your company. Put this forth in terms of a movie that you are watching of what has happened, even though you are looking into the future. It actually works.

Then work out your master plan. That comes in two steps. You need to work out the strategy for your company. Where are you going and what is wise for you to accomplish? As part of the strategy, comes the tactical steps which is your strategy broken down into doable steps. This is like saying you want to take that hill, or that island as a strategy, and now you have to break that down into actions to do. Those are the tactical steps and the most important part of developing your own visionary mindset and improving your strategic thinking capabilities.

Now with those steps all fleshed out, you need a 30-60-90 day plan of actions to income. By this I mean you need to generate more revenue that fast through the implementation of your master plan. This is especially useful if you are a startup, or you are beginning a new division, product, or service in your company.

And now the last step, the eighth step in this visionary mindset process: take those actions from your tactical plan and your 30-60-90 day plan and write out what you need to do today. What does your company need to do today? What do your employees need to do today? Write those out and distribute to those responsible.

It is by the execution of those steps that your company will generate the revenue that it needs in order to sustain itself, pay the payroll, purchase the raw goods, and so forth, to survive and then thrive. Make sure that affiliates, subs, consultants, and anyone that works with your company know about the top three items of this list. They need to know what page you are on and that will give them the wherewithal to help you as best as they can.

ABOUT THE AUTHOR

A Top 100 Apple Podcast, the #1 show on Chartable world-wide (June 2022), and #1 on VoiceAmerica (over five years running), The Tony DUrso Show is routinely in the Top Ten internationally in various categories.

Launched in 2015 as Revenue Chat Radio, and eventually as The Tony DUrso Show on VoiceAmerica, Tony interviews elite entrepreneurs including Jack Canfield, Mark Victor Hansen, Kevin Harrington, and Wesley Snipes.

With over 40 million total listens, The Tony DUrso Show provides a massive impact for entrepreneurs who want to share with the world. In addition to weekly interviews, Tony's company provides social media marketing to help anyone gain more social media followers and grow their podcast. (Proper spelling is D'Urso, but as search engines get confused, the apostrophe is dropped to make it simpler.)

THE MAGIC OF DISCOVERING YOUR GENIUS

SHELBY JO LONG

When I was seventeen, I was in a car accident that put me into a coma. When I came out of the coma, my left arm and left leg were paralyzed. The right side of my brain was impacted in the car accident. Even though I was wearing my seatbelt, my body was thrown toward the passenger side with such force that I bruised the right side of my brain. Because the right side of your brain controls the left side of your body, I was left partially paralyzed after I woke from the coma.

During my four weeks in the rehabilitation center, I had to relearn many unconscious/automatic physical and mental acts we do daily, like holding a pencil, writing on a piece of paper, holding a fork, and placing one foot in front of the other. I even had to remember how to swallow. My brain didn't remember those simple acts we take for granted daily. My rehabilitation would be focused on relearning these basic functions.

The big question was, *Would I ever walk again?*

My physical therapy sessions focused on relearning the function of my legs so I could walk again. I remember training extensively in the pool, which allowed me to focus on how my legs were supposed to move before I put any weight on them. We trained for weeks as I rebuilt my strength and muscle control in hopes I could walk again.

The doctors had said I could go home to visit my friends and family for our Fourth of July celebration—if I was physically mobile and could walk independently. That became the motivation I needed to get out of the hospital. I was determined.

Two and a half weeks into my recovery is burned in my memory: *Today is the day.* My therapists pushed my wheelchair into the long hallway. All the weeks of strength training and walking in the pool led to this moment. I braced myself against my wheelchair arms. I stood up.

Then, I had to think through the action of taking each step. The visualization happened first, then I had to think about the physical act of placing one foot in front of the other, and then I needed the internal confidence to think about my successful walk down the hallway even before I put one foot in front of the other.

I took those first steps on my own without any device or therapist helping me; it was such an important moment for me. This was the action that would help me earn my independence again. I would no longer have to rely on others to help me get out of bed or walk across the room. I could do these things on my own. And I could go home for the Fourth of July weekend.

After I took those first steps, my muscle memory began to kick in, and my physical recovery went quickly.

The evolution of my brain's recovery wasn't as easy to pinpoint. I didn't/couldn't recognize or remember the changes in how I processed information because the changes were happening so quickly. So, the physical act of standing up and recognizing that my brain had to tell my feet to take steps seemed like one of my biggest accomplishments in the weeks since the accident. Overcoming this huge barrier gave a great boost to my internal confidence.

I felt the same excitement and confidence when my children took their first steps. Because with those steps, they became independent in a new way after months of crawling and relying on others.

Leveraging Your Innate Genius

When I integrated the knowledge I had from my past with my new way of understanding the world around me, I could forge a path forward. But I couldn't have taken those steps unless I understood where I was and how to approach the new challenge.

Stated another way: When I integrated my muscle memory from the past with the techniques I learned in physical therapy, I could step forward in an entirely new way. Similarly, I could forge a path forward by integrating my pre-accident identity with my new way of understanding the world around me. But I couldn't have taken those steps unless I understood where I was and had the tools I needed to approach the new challenge.

When you step out into your business, internal awareness and confidence are key to establishing a foundation for yourself. They are also key when establishing relationships with your employees and customers.

It all goes back to the foundation and basics. When I took those first steps out of the wheelchair, it was the basic movement of consciously placing one foot in front of the other that was a necessary foundation for taking a few steps, walking across the room, or even rejoining the track team during my senior year of high school. A solid foundation is the basic building block for gaining strength, building confidence, and preparing for the next stage.

I sought a comfortable foundation in other areas of my recovery as well.

I didn't understand my genius then, but after my trauma, I gravitated toward the skills that felt second nature to me. I was passionate about returning to the activity of debate because I enjoyed the quick responses, speaking, and competitive atmosphere. Little did I know that these skills would help me recover from my TBI and become important skills and background for my journey as an entrepreneur.

My ability to create concise and memorable messages in my speeches is a foundational skill in my business branding and program development. My ability to create summaries and conclusions from the combination of different perspectives and research is foundational for my teaching and program development. My ability to speak in front of different audiences is a foundational skill that helps me with sales and presentation skills. Reflecting upon the practices that were second nature from my education and debate competition became the foundation for my genius behind my business.

Build a strong foundation to serve as your platform for growth and expansion. Do what is natural to you, and then remember the steps of how you arrived at your genius. Your genius is in your muscle memory and your intuition.

DISCOVERY OF GENIUS

So, how do you discover your genius? A period of self-reflection and deep thought about the processes that are second nature to you is where you can begin to discover your genius. A simple SWOT analysis will help you discover your strengths in your genius arsenal so you can help solve problems for others. Questions that can help you begin to identify your genius include:

- What do you enjoy about your work?
- What activities have you gravitated toward in your spare time?
- What was your favorite subject in school?
- What sets you apart from others in the workplace?

Think of the problem you solve with your genius. You discovered a process in your work and life journey that changed how you live or operate your business. This transformative process has created a more fulfilling work or home life for you and helped you enjoy your time more. This transformation journey is foundational to your approach to solving problems and creating balance in your life. This small step is part of your intuition and is second nature to you. It is your genius. And it can be used to help others solve a business or lifestyle challenge they may have.

A Specific Solution is the Path to Monetization

There are many problems in the world, and challenges keep compounding for businesses with the changes in the economy and the stresses of the pandemic. You don't need to solve all the business challenges for people; you just need to solve one. And when you solve one, and you're really good at solving one problem, that's where you can monetize your genius. You home in on that one specific concept, and that concept will make you money. It will also allow you to expand your influence into other things. You are the genius, the expert, and the authority helping others solve their challenges.

You just have to solve *one* problem.

You don't have to solve all the problems. You have to solve one. And people will seek you out for that. Then, your power increases because your credibility increases. Additionally, your prices can increase because you solve that problem so well and efficiently that people will knock down your door. That's what I want to be for academics, experts, and coaches who want to monetize their expertise and are ready for that because that adds so much credibility to your brand. That adds credibility, force, and intellectual property that people are looking for; it also adds background and differentiates you to those looking for your expertise.

There are a lot of entrepreneurs and business coaches for entrepreneurs out there. I see the advertisements all the time. I know there's a lot of competition, but I also know that if I'm saying the right things to the right community, that's what's going to make a difference.

In business, we often want to serve whomever we can because we have a huge audience. That's like throwing shit at a wall and seeing what sticks. It's hard to do that. You can build the business that way, but for solo entrepreneurs, the challenge is being specific and solving those problems. You can speak to everybody worldwide, but we have these platforms to reach people. There is incredible opportunity and reach with your genius idea, and the more specific you are, the more valuable your genius becomes.

We don't call a general contractor to draw up plans for our house; we call an architect because they have the training and expertise to do the job. We visit an optometrist rather than a general practitioner when we need to have our eyes checked. We work with marketing companies rather than website developers when we want to increase traffic to our website. Consumers seek specific services all the time. Why should your genius be any different?

KNOW YOUR AUDIENCE

Your business brand and brand story are critical to have in place as you transition your skills to a new audience. Genius doesn't just exist in a bubble; there are competitors to consider and resources to understand in the marketplace. Many small businesses don't consider their surroundings while developing their business launch and marketing. I've seen many entrepreneurs, myself included, who have developed businesses in a vacuum. I have the pieces in place. I have my mailing list. I have my messages. I have all these things set in place, but I haven't considered my environment, the competition, or how I differentiate myself. Your brand and brand story separate your genius solution from your competition.

That lesson has been embedded in my consciousness since my debate days. I could have a great argument, but my message will fall flat if I'm not considering what they're saying in the opposition, the response to that argument, or the competition I have. I must have a dynamic understanding and engagement in the moment. The same principles are true for entrepreneurs of genius business solutions. Unless there is an understanding of the landscape of competition, your idea won't stand out in the noise of marketing.

Market analysis is key. If you're opening a restaurant in a busy restaurant section, you must analyze your market and understand why people would choose your restaurant over somebody else's. The same is true in this digital economy, where we have to tell our stories to connect with potential clients emotionally to stand out from the competition.

Your brand story is the most powerful tool in marketing your business. Consumers buy brands they trust because they are emotionally connected to the story. I help my clients think about their image, what they're promoting, their message, and whether that message is right for their audience.

Your genius is unique and different, but when you tell the story behind your genius, you create an influential and memorable brand that differentiates you from your competitors.

TRUST IN YOURSELF

A digital stamp of your business is necessary in this marketplace. Your brand and emotional connection to your business are more important in today's business world than ever. Clarity in your brand identity is critical for connecting with your audience in the digital space. However, the performance and communication of your brand in the marketplace differentiate your business from your competitors.

Your brand identity message is key because it explains who you are. The message of your brand promise is also critical as you begin to monetize your genius because it helps you clarify your customer journey. Your genius will transform the experience of your clients. If they have a clear picture of your brand journey before they even talk to you, they can understand what to anticipate when working with you. Your brand promise is about the client journey and results. When clearly outlined to your audience, your brand promise helps set your business apart from competitors in the marketplace.

The messages we use in our businesses are the language that creates a connection with our audience. When the audience understands your genius can help solve a problem they may have in their business, your value proposition becomes clear, and you can begin to create a change for your clients. Your brand story will connect an audience emotionally to your brand and your journey. Your brand promise will clarify the results your audience can anticipate when working with you.

My experience draws me to the competition of entrepreneurship and how businesses connect with audiences. This speaks to my experience in debate. We debate about different subjects every time. The audience is different every time we debate. It's dynamic. You must move, shift, and adjust what you're saying to be persuasive with different audiences. This is also true for monetizing your genius. You have the basic principles with your promise but can adapt with coaching and consulting.

I want to help more people, and I want to help solve more problems. I also want people to be successful; that's in my nature. That's why I'm a teacher. There's a new platform now. However, I didn't discover until later in my teaching career that I could make the same impact with business owners that I did with students.

COMPETITION DRIVES PERSONAL AND PROFESSIONAL GROWTH

I enjoyed the personal growth of the activities I participated in, but these were also communities where I felt comfortable and could grow personally and professionally. The competitive drive I homed in collegiate debate applied directly to my journey into the business world.

When I began my competitive years in collegiate debate, I found myself surrounded by many talented competitors with vast experiences and backgrounds. This competitive yet cooperative environment pushed me to practice and hone my skills to be at the same level as my colleagues, friends, and debate adversaries. Strangely, this comfort zone of talent, criticism, adversarial conversations, and deep knowledge became a space for my recovery and personal development. I worked hard to have this talented world of debate be a part of my identity in college.

But we all had that background and experience, which made us more isolated but stronger in the community. When we talk about rhetoric studies, it makes sense. We develop language, understanding, and meanings within groups. And we talk about how these groups, like families and sports teams, have this language and understanding that's formed between them. And it connects us and helps us create meaning, but it also keeps people out.

My experience in debate then became significantly bigger than just the competition because the competition helped me discover—or remember—the way to think. All the synapses came firing again. Additionally, this community was so large and influential in helping students learn how to speak and communicate better and more efficiently, which makes your writing better; it makes everything better.

I also spent time in Ireland, which greatly influenced my future of debate because I looked at debate as much more than a competitive tool; it was also a tool for personal growth.

This combination of inspiration, intimidation, and competition became such a familiar spot/comfort zone/cornerstone of my identity that I decided to follow the career path of inspiring other students to be in the competitive debate world where they would grow professionally and personally.

I found the same type of competitive environment on my entrepreneurial journey. Business is competitive. We are surrounded by so much talent and experience and ever-expanding opportunities. The competition for our business has only increased with new technology and the push to have an online element in our business in the post-pandemic world. Entrepreneurs who tell their story, connect with their intended audience, and differentiate their business from their competition will build a solid and sustainable foundation for their businesses. Your genius is positioned as a promise to help your clients through a transformative journey.

Monetizing Your Genius

Deciding to move your genius to a new space has everything to do with your mindset. You confront the fear of the unknown and explore new opportunities for your knowledge outside of a space where you have grown personally and professionally. You enter a space without establishing authority or credibility for your ideas or approach. Fear of rejection, failure, and judgment are all familiar feelings when your genius journey begins. However, your confidence in your experience and strengths will help you pivot to meet the needs of your target audience.

This change is significantly more challenging when you have created a product or process out of the genius you have taken so long to develop in your professional career and education. Your years of experience behind your genius and the passion that has driven you to help solve problems for other people are embedded in your program. Your program is an extension of your genius, so your offer for your new audience is more vulnerable.

My experience in adapting my expertise happened in two professional contexts. When I began teaching at the college level, I discovered the communication confidence and style I had developed through my years in collegiate speech and debate needed to be altered so I could serve the students with my knowledge. I had spent four years on the Carroll College debate team, surrounded by the nation's top coaching talent and student competitors. We were National Champions during my senior year in college. This talent influenced my communication style in addition to helping me develop confidence in my communication skills.

The confidence and communication style I developed over my years of debating in high school and college were foundational for my teaching career. My confidence in speaking became important in my teaching. The quick preparation and argumentation theory focus in debate influenced my teaching approach. However, I developed some skills in my competitive speaking career that I needed to adjust as I stepped into my teaching career.

I needed to be the content authority to influence students in the classroom. I needed a short-term and long-term plan on how I would run each class in addition to the content presentation throughout the fifteen-week term. My communication style had to move from the concise, brief, and argumentative style of speaking to an educational and storytelling style of communication. Transitioning from a limited preparation for my seven-minute speech in a debate round to planning the content I would present for a ninety-minute class period took planning and adaptation.

The second time I experienced this transition was when I began consulting with organizations and conducting my digital course. I had been teaching business communication at the college level for ten years, so I felt that transitioning to this new audience would be relatively fast. I ran live seminars and training sessions in businesses and my first digital program. I quickly learned I needed to adapt my communication style to this new audience.

Instead of teaching my new audience about foundations and theory, I needed to focus on applying communication principles to daily work practices. I needed to sell the idea to my new audience and explore what kind of differences these principles could make in the workplace. I needed to discuss the return on investment of communication training for organizations. I needed to make my teaching much more focused on the needs of the business. So, I changed my communication style to match the audience's needs. And my communication became much clearer and focused on solving the needs of the audience. I provide action and solutions and empower my clients to move in a direction to make their work more efficient and enjoyable.

So, how do you transform your genius to a new audience?

Your genius begins to gain value when it is situated with an audience. A clear vision of who you serve and how your genius serves their needs in their work or lifestyle will allow you to monetize your process. A clear understanding of the target market for your services is critical in this process.

A clear understanding of your audience's demographics is key to establishing your communication and marketing strategy. The basic demographics like age and profession are key in this process so you can plan how you will communicate with your clients before, during, and after the service journey. These demographics are also key for you to understand how the psychological needs of your target audience are where you can begin to frame your genius as the path for your audience to achieve success or achievement in their business. Understanding these needs of your target audience will help you create more compelling messages in your marketing and give you a competitive advantage in the marketplace. A few questions to clarify your offer for your new audience include:

- What are the goals your target market seeks?
- What problems do they experience in their lives or workplaces that challenge them to achieve more profit in their businesses?

- What would help your clients gain more profit in their businesses?
- What solution would create more time or ease for their businesses or lives?

These deeper questions will give you a distinct understanding of the problem you solve and what type of value that has in a business.

Finally, create a clear path between your new target audience and the problem you can solve for them. Focus on who is in your audience so you clearly understand how your genius is an irreplaceable service for your audience. Knowing who is in your new target audience is critical to how you will construct and deliver the message to those who need your expertise. As a genius entrepreneur, the match between the problem you solve and the audience who needs your solution is the key to monetizing the service of your genius.

Clarity in the niche you serve, the problem you solve, and the impact of your solution is the magic of transforming your expertise.

Identifying a clear niche audience keeps you in your zone for your ideal clients. It allows you to deepen your client relationships to develop a strong return and referral service for your business. You also stay in your space of innovation and creativity, where you can test offers with your client community and create more solutions within your group.

Think of an accountant who helps with bookkeeping, taxes, and financial planning for small businesses. Good accountants make themselves indispensable to small businesses because they meet multiple levels of needs for business owners. They identify an audience, create solutions to problems with their tools and resources, and invest in long-term client relationships. The real estate agent you remember will not only help you find your house, but they will also walk you through the entire client journey of selling your current house, identifying the neighborhood and school district in which you want to live, and direct you toward financing and contractor resources. They help you solve many challenges you may confront when buying and selling a house.

Your genius has the same opportunity. You solve problems. You also provide expert support and connections to resources that may assist in other potential business challenges.

Your genius's magic is adapting to your new audience and creating a community surrounding your ideas.

You must decide to invest time to discover a new space.

Transformative Mindset

Entrepreneurship in itself is a journey. There are ups and downs in the economy; consumer behaviors change, and it is challenging to have consistency in your production and service. You need to mentally prepare yourself for these challenges in addition to the lack of engagement or even rejection of your ideas in the marketplace. You must be prepared to pivot your approach and respond to the needs of the audience that is the target of your solution. That is why careful construction of your genius, an execution plan, and the ability to adapt your communication style to new challenges are critical for your genius journey.

Magic: When your genius serves as the foundation for you to create solutions for others.

Your Intuition

The true magic of creation emerges in your genius program when you allow yourself to follow your intuition. The processes you gravitate toward daily and the foundational skills that emerge in your workspace are developed through practice in different business contexts. These often take deep reflection or a third party to help you realize your full potential.

STEPPING INTO YOU

An example from my business experience and reflection on my skills is in my messaging. My years as a college professor, debate participant, and coach have helped me focus on the skill of developing concise and memorable messages. If you don't draw your audience's attention to the important takeaways from your speech, your main points will not resonate with your audience. You become much more influential in your communication with clear, concise, and impactful messages that call attention to the value of your message with the audience.

Intuition also manifests in instant synergy in business partnerships. When you are confident with your skills, offer, and genius, others will be drawn to your business. You will attract leads and draw others into your business partnerships. Synergy creates the potential for business partnerships that can change the landscape of your business reach.

TAPPING INTO YOUR CREATIVITY

As you discover and monetize your genius, you allow yourself to step into a place of empowered creation. You are integrating your ingrained skills into how you make decisions and influence others. This is your unique power and, ultimately, your selling proposition. When these talents become the center of your genius offer, you create a bigger impact on your clients and a more fulfilled career and life.

When you build a business that operates in your zone of genius, a true connection is made between your passion and career. The fulfillment you experience as your work in your genius has an incredible influence on your clients and business partners. You will attract people to your business and operate in a confidence that only emerges when you work in a space created by your professional strengths. This is where you will have the most impact.

Your Genius—The Journey of Your Expertise

What happens when you begin to run your business inside your zone of genius? You are in a zone of creation. As you guide others through your genius idea, you will gain the ability to adapt and transform your expertise to serve your clients at a higher level. Guiding your clients through the journey of your expertise allows both parties to be empowered to excel beyond expectations throughout the journey. As the expert, you will serve and guide in an equally fulfilling journey.

Create new ways to solve problems, share your experiences with others, and empower your clients to transform their lives and tap into their genius.

There is personal power in your genius.

There is transformative power in your genius.

Your genius can create opportunities for you, your business, and your clients.

Solving Problems for Others

You can persuade when your audience identifies with you.

Two key concepts of identification emerge consistently in the classes I teach as well as in the work I do with small businesses—the academic concepts of identification and the enthymeme.

Kenneth Burke, a literary theorist, talks about the concept of identification as a critical piece to creating a connection with your audience. *When the speaker identifies with the values and needs of the audience, the stage is set for persuasion and the exchange of information.*

Because I teach human communication, human interaction, and organizational communication, everything I talk about in the classroom and teach students applies to real-life situations. That's also what business is. This created an opportunity for me to start a business, or at least I felt an opportunity to create a business out of what I saw was needed. All those human interaction elements are needed to run and promote a business and to make it, especially in the digital age. It has become even more important that your message connects to the right audience. These are all the basic pieces that I teach in the classroom and are taught in writing classrooms.

And I think that's in my nature, too. I'm a speaker. I've been speaking all my life, and debate connects with this because debate is similar. I was in the world of debate. I spoke the language of debate, but the only people who understood that were the people in debate. When I was coaching my team, it became more important for me to concentrate on the skills, community, and learning that happened outside of just winning debate rounds. The application and distribution of that knowledge became more important to me. So, we hosted campus debates frequently, and I took that knowledge elsewhere and made it a part of my program.

I initially had the roots of speaking, but it was conversation that happened in a bubble. Then, I wanted that bubble not to burst; I wanted it to go further, to reach larger audiences, which set the stage for me to get into organizational communication and dig into the branding of people and businesses and the importance of a very clear message about who you are, who you serve, and how you can help.

And those are key pieces to creating your brand and distributing your expertise to a larger audience. And that's the basis of the program that I have now with the expertise part because we experts live in this area, but yes, we're comfortable here. We know how to speak the language. We know how to do all the things. Some people do lead generation; some write books; some focus on accounting or whatever their expertise is. I figure out how to communicate that expertise to others and help other people discover:

- How to use that expertise themselves
- How to sell their products
- How to productize when they must reach a larger audience

This is all foundational. I started to think about the possibilities of knowledge and expertise, how those can help and empower other people, and how to present it all in a coaching manner rather than a consulting manner.

Building Trust with a New Audience

As I began my entrepreneurial journey, I felt the tension of identification with audiences. I realized I had become so entrenched in the academic system or group that it became challenging to think of a life outside that group. I had spent my academic career writing for an academic audience, so the habits and behaviors became a part of my processing and thinking.

The speaking habits I developed as a debate competitor, debate coach, and lecturer in a classroom did not necessarily meet the needs of the new audience I spoke to. I was comfortable with my speaking and training skill set. Still, I had to work to establish that trusting relationship with my new audience, to create that *identification* so we would connect as people and share my thoughts and teaching.

I had the knowledge, research, and experience, yet I was in a space where I needed to think about how to bridge that gap with my new audience. In a period of transition and movement in my career and communication habits and skills, I felt like an academic refugee.

Regarding communication, lecturing is a completely different way of teaching than an advising session. Both happened, but I became used to lecturing. I like to be in front of the audience. My classes were an hour and a half long, so I usually went in with a game plan. And I had no problem filling that time, but entrepreneur teaching needs to be much more structured. People don't have time to sit in a class and listen to the foundational theories of Aristotle and Kenneth Burke.

That also depends on if I'm working with other coaches. They may want that long process. However, some businesses just want quick answers. It all depends on the client's needs. More information is not necessarily good, right? It's the right information. And it's the engagement and the right information that is good, which also goes back to debate. You have a very limited amount of time to make an impact on somebody. And we've all sat through training sessions thinking, *Is this going to be over soon?*

That's not the kind of coach I want to be. I want to be a coach who is active and engaged. I don't want a one-and-done relationship. I want a continued relationship because as you grow as an entrepreneur, I want to continue that journey. After all, there are multiple levels. You start your business, and then you grow your business. And then, when you scale your business, there are constant challenges along the way. It's not just writing a business plan, and then you're good for a couple of years. No, because you write a business plan and you have some ideas about what you will do. But then you open, and the pandemic hits, you must pay taxes, or another challenge arises. There is a constant movement and fluidity that we must be aware of. It's not concrete; it's not black and white.

What works for Tony Robbins will not work for me because I'm a different person. I have different qualities. I have a different way of engaging. I can't do those big events anymore, but someday, I will. I'm speaking only for me. I'm not speaking for other academics, but there's a lot of consulting. For instance, the environmental studies professors may work with the State's Land Grant Institute. There are a lot of other opportunities for that. But transforming your expertise into a product is a challenge. And it is speaking to a different audience, and it's monetizing what you have and figuring out a way that that can be consumed.

COMMUNITY

Community and mentorship became a significant part of my recovery and career and had a tremendous influence on the formation of my business. Community and developing and refining ideas within a brand and a program that is developed also became central to engaging my clients.

When I decided to create my business, I realized many things I didn't know about business. It was interesting and frustrating to me that I had all this experience with business communi cation and persuasion and was training the next generation of business owners in the college environment. Still, I quickly discovered there was so much to learn when engaging in a new environment. I was no longer the teacher of the information; I was the student. I had to learn business practices, sales tactics, money management, online marketing techniques, and countless other business elements.

I heard of mastermind sessions where I could hear how people were doing things. I think that's great. Maybe I'll try that. And to make those connections or to reach out. Even in our mastermind, we use each other's skills, which I think is great and expanding. And I would like to provide that environment for academics, too, because I don't have all the answers. When you get a group of us together, there's a whole lot of smart people who have a whole lot of ideas to think about how they can make a product out of their knowledge. They have this knowledge that they spend so much time cultivating, and they're often published. They're successful in this realm but also have power outside of that.

I had no idea how to find new mentors and a new community in a new field, but I trusted they would show up. There was something else out there for me, a place where I could use my skills and find more fulfillment in my career.

One of the things I learned during my exploration is that finding mentors and community in the entrepreneurial space is challenging. Still, if you trust who you are and know the problems you can solve, a community will be attracted to you, your business, your brand, and your offer.

First, you can read all the inspiring business books out there. However, nothing is as valuable as being in a community of people experiencing similar challenges in their business development process. A community is key to learning the different business practices, resources, and how to get things done in your new industry. It's also where you'll likely find informal mentors who will show you the ropes, although you may also wish to hire a coach or consultant.

Second, your community can help your business grow in many different ways. They can also support your business development, function as a beta group, and potentially become long-term customers. When you have built a community around your business's vision and mission, they will be a support network as you continue to refine your business model and adjust to the needs of the marketplace and your clients/target market. When you are in a trusted community with other entrepreneurs, you can bounce ideas off each other and use each other as sounding boards.

Third, community provides support and momentum for your business. It will also show you the path to transform your intellectual property into a product ready for the marketplace.

Community is central to my business model because the discourse and problem-solving that happens during a group conversation cannot be matched. When multiple people share their unique perspectives and the ideas build upon each other, the magic of group creativity is realized. (My live business mastermind sessions developed out of this idea. While I direct the conversation, the advice is built out of the perspective of every member.)

Community is central to building your business.

ABOUT THE AUTHOR

A professional speaker, international speaking coach, and four-time international best-selling author, Shelby Jo Long is a recognized expert in corporate communications.

Shelby is also CEO of Business Dynamics and CEO of Rogue Publishing Partners, where she helps visionaries develop an infrastructure for their business and influence. Her particular method helps ingenious entrepreneurs position their idea in the marketplace. Her bestselling book, *I See Your Genius: Transform Your Idea Into Income*, is a valuable reference and guide for entrepreneurs.

Besides her leadership roles, Shelby is currently a tenured professor of business communication. Her background in business culture, communication, and leadership has earned her a reputation as an expert in the field. Shelby's expertise in corporate culture and leadership helps create a strong framework for small business success.

Shelby's tireless dedication, extensive knowledge of corporate communications, and passion for helping organizations build a solid brand and framework make her an indispensable asset to both the strategic advisor board and the organizations she serves.

The Importance of Vision and Innovation in Disruptive Leadership

Julie Ducharme

Visionary and traditional CEOs exhibit different leadership styles and approaches, each with its own characteristics. When we look at some of the greats out there, Jeff Bezos, Steve Jobs, Bill Gates, Elon Musk, and Sara Blakley, each has seen tremendous success. However, their leadership styles vary greatly. One might ask how they can have such different leadership styles but still arrive at such a high level of success as a visionary leader.

Vision and Innovation

Each one of the men and women I mentioned above could see the vision and big picture and set ambitious long-term goals for themselves and their companies. All were also breaking into their industries or disrupting the industries. There was no manual, and no one who came before them to give them some tips on success. They were figuring out how to lead and what to lead and documented their failures just as much as their success. Why? Because failures matter when you are searching for success. In their question to change their industry, they had a clear vision for the future. These men and women were known for constantly seeking innovative ways to achieve their goals. Traditional CEOs, on the other hand, tend to focus more on maintaining the status quo, optimizing current processes, and meeting short-term targets.

RISK-TAKING

When I first started as a CEO, I was not much of a risk-taker. I was what you would call a calculated risk-taker. In hindsight, this slowed my journey because I was cautious. A visionary CEO is more willing to take risks to pursue their bold vision. They understand that innovation and growth often come with risks and are willing to step out of their comfort zones. And I eventually realized if I was going to push my companies forward, I needed to step out of my comfort zone as well.

ADAPTABILITY

Another key characteristic of visionary CEOs is being adaptable and open to change. My leadership style is very much focused on being an adaptive leader. Adapting and changing happen daily in all my companies. If you can't adapt, you will be left behind as your competitors do. As a CEO, I had to understand the importance of evolving with the rapidly changing business landscape and be willing to pivot strategies when necessary.

Thirty years ago, a traditional CEO might be more resistant to change, preferring tried-and-true methods even in the face of shifting market dynamics. One of my favorite things is to watch documentaries on companies that did not want to take a chance on something. Later, they see that person or company they rejected become a billion-dollar company. We always make jokes about why we didn't get stock in Yahoo back in the day. Because we didn't have the vision to see the possibilities. The difference between traditional and innovative CEOs is the ability to adapt and see the vision.

LONG-TERM FOCUS

Part of being a visionary CEO is prioritizing long-term growth and sustainability. All the billionaires I mentioned above were in it for the long run—about 20 years—before they saw their vision take flight. They were willing to do the grind, deal with the failures, and keep going because they had their long-term goal in sight. I always remember the story of Steve Jobs desperately trying to get bank funding. They thought his computer idea was absurd, but he kept going in the face of that because he could see the long-term value of the vision of the company. Traditional CEOs often are more focused on short-term profitability and may not prioritize investments that don't show immediate returns.

EMPLOYEE ENGAGEMENT

There have been many conversations about Steve Jobs and his controversial leadership style. Still, when you look at visionary CEOs, they often emphasize a strong company culture, employee empowerment, and a sense of purpose. Despite Steve Jobs' odd and sometimes inappropriate leadership, he created company culture, empowered employees, and provided a sense of purpose to his people. That is why they stayed. People often said they were so dedicated it was like a cult at Apple. Visionary CEOS inspire their teams to align with the company's vision and feel passionate about their work.

MARKET DISRUPTION

Market disruption is a key aspect of any visionary CEO. Each of the leaders above was creating a market disruption to existing or new markets with groundbreaking products or services. Their goal was to create new opportunities and redefine industries. Traditional CEOs might focus on incremental improvements to existing products and services without radically changing the competitive landscape.

COMMUNICATION AND STORYTELLING

Storytelling is one of the most powerful ways you can communicate with your employees as a visionary CEO. Storytelling brings people together; it finds an emotional connection. Visionary CEOs are pros at this and excel at communication and storytelling. They can articulate their vision in a compelling way that resonates with employees, investors, and customers, fostering a sense of purpose and excitement. If you have listened to any of these CEOs I mentioned above, you can see that as they speak. Their stories are powerful and resonate with many. Traditional CEOs may have more transactional communication styles, focusing on facts and figures rather than crafting a narrative around the company's journey.

In today's business world, where technology is rapidly reshaping industries and market dynamics are constantly evolving, the characteristics of a visionary CEO are essential for several reasons. With innovation and adaptation, visionary CEOs are better equipped to navigate and capitalize on technological advancements, industry disruptions, and changing consumer preferences. Their willingness to innovate ensures the company remains relevant and competitive. It is important for visionary CEOs to focus on long-term strategies that position the company for sustained success, even in uncertain times. This long-term perspective helps the company weather economic fluctuations and market shifts.

Developing a Compelling Vision

Developing a compelling vision for an organization is a critical task for a CEO. A clear and inspiring vision provides direction, purpose, and motivation for employees, investors, and other stakeholders. Here is a seven-step process I used as a CEO to develop a compelling vision and understand its impact on overall company strategy.

First, the CEO must understand the current state of the industry, market, and company. Before envisioning the future, a CEO should deeply understand the company's current strengths, weaknesses, market position, and industry trends. This analysis helps in identifying the gaps that the vision can address.

The second important step for creating a vision is understanding and engaging stakeholders. The CEO needs to involve key stakeholders such as employees, customers, investors, and industry experts in the vision development process. Their insights and perspectives can provide valuable input and ensure the vision resonates with all parties.

The third step is to define a clear purpose. A compelling vision should answer the question, "Why does the organization exist?" It should articulate the company's purpose beyond just making profits and explain how it aims to positively impact its customers, employees, and the world.

The fourth step is to be ambitious and inspirational. I don't think this can be taught; I think it is built into leaders. A visionary CEO should think big and set ambitious goals that challenge the status quo. The vision should inspire employees to strive for excellence and feel excited about future possibilities.

The fifth step is aligned with the core values of the company and your core values as a person. You can't be a visionary if the core values don't resonate with you. I think every great visionary CEO's core values align with the vision of what they are doing. It does for me. I can't work with a company that does not embody the same values as me. The vision should be aligned with the company's core values and culture. It should reflect the organization's identity and what it stands for, ensuring authenticity and coherence.

The sixth step is to consider industry trends and disruptions. A visionary CEO should have an eye on industry trends and potential disruptions. The vision should consider how the company can position itself to lead in a changing market landscape. The CEO should also visualize the future after looking at these trends and paint a vivid picture of the future when the vision is realized. This helps employees and stakeholders see the potential impact of their efforts and feel a stronger sense of purpose.

The seventh step is to communicate effectively. Any leader needs this skill—not just CEOs. Having a compelling vision must be communicated clearly and consistently across the organization. CEOs should use various communication channels and storytelling techniques (as mentioned above) to ensure the vision resonates with everyone.

Finally, the creation of the vision should be looked at to see if it fosters adaptability. This means a vision should be inspirational yet adaptable. The business environment can change rapidly, so the vision should allow flexibility while maintaining the core purpose.

Strategic alignment is critical for the vision to impact company strategy. The vision acts as a guiding principle that aligns all aspects of the company's strategy, ensuring that every decision and initiative moves toward the desired future state. The other aspect that needs to be considered is innovation. How does the vision encourage a culture of innovation by challenging employees to think creatively and develop solutions that align with the visionary goals?

Another important aspect is how the vision helps prioritize resource allocation. Investments, projects, and initiatives that contribute directly to the vision are prioritized. Does the vision create a compelling vision that attracts top talent who are motivated to contribute to something meaningful? Does the vision set the company apart from competitors? And when the business landscape evolves, can the vision serve as a constant reference point? It helps the company adapt to changes while staying true to its long-term objectives.

A compelling vision is a foundational element that informs and shapes the entire company strategy. It sets the tone for innovation, growth, and long-term success while providing a sense of purpose and direction for everyone involved in the organization.

BALANCING RISK-TAKING AND INNOVATION

Balancing innovation and risk-taking with maintaining stability and sustainable growth is a complex challenge that visionary CEOs face. Successfully managing this balance requires strategic thinking, careful planning, and effective execution. Here's how a visionary CEO can approach this balancing act.

- Set a clear vision and strategy

- Foster a culture of innovation

- Assess and manage risks

- Differentiate between core and adjacent innovations

- Allocate resources strategically

- Recognize incremental vs. disruptive innovation

- Test and validate

- Embrace agile methodologies

- Diversify revenue streams

- Monitor and measure progress

- Long-term vs. short-term focus

- Remain flexible and adaptable

- Communicate effectively and transparently

To take risks and bring innovation, you must cultivate a company culture that encourages experimentation, creativity, and continuous improvement. Any time this is implemented, the risk becomes higher. A visionary CEO must weigh the risk and see what they are willing to lose if it doesn't work. Google is great at implementing this idea because they allow people to work on their project ideas during work. If they come up with something amazing, Google offers to buy them out or make them a partner. The brilliance of this is there is little risk because they are not working on an official project for Google. The worst thing that happens is that they lose some work time of employees, but the culture of innovation allows for this.

As a leader, you need to distinguish between entrepreneurship and intrapreneurship. These affect core innovations. Risk can't happen with our resources, and CEOs need to allocate resources based on a balanced portfolio approach. Dedicate a portion of resources to high-risk, high-reward initiatives while investing in projects that ensure steady growth and stability.

Before scaling an innovative idea, test it in a controlled environments to validate its feasibility and potential impact. This approach helps reduce the risk associated with scaling unproven concepts. Additionally, work to implement agile methodologies that enable rapid iteration and adaptation. This approach can be particularly useful for managing innovation while maintaining flexibility in the face of changing market conditions. Establish key performance indicators (KPIs) that track the success of both innovative and stable initiatives. Regularly review and assess these metrics to ensure the organization is on track to achieve its goals. Stay open to adjusting strategies based on market feedback and changing conditions. Flexibility allows course correction if an innovative approach doesn't yield the expected results.

Balancing innovation and risk-taking with stability and sustainable growth requires a dynamic approach that evolves over time. A visionary CEO should be prepared to make difficult decisions, pivot strategies when needed, and find ways to synergize innovation efforts with the company's core operations. By carefully managing these elements, a visionary CEO can create an environment where innovation propels the organization forward while maintaining a solid foundation for long-term success.

EXPERIENCES SHAPE YOU AS A VISIONARY CEO

My two oldest businesses are 23 and 25 years old. When I reflect on how my experiences helped shape me into a visionary CEO, I think, Where do I start? As a retired high-level athlete, I spent many years playing sports at a high level, and frankly, I am an adrenaline junky. When I switched over to owning my companies, the grit, courage, and determination I learned from sports transferred into being an entrepreneur. I love going after those big deals and then nailing them. This helped drive me to be a visionary CEO.

HOW DO VISIONARY CEOS CULTIVATE A GROWTH MINDSET?

Cultivating a growth mindset and fostering a culture of continuous learning and improvement within an organization requires intentional effort from the CEO and leadership team. Here are steps a CEO can take to achieve this.

It is important that CEOs embody a growth mindset themselves. Demonstrate a willingness to learn, adapt, and embrace challenges. We must lead by example. Let your people see that you have failed and how you learned from it. Failure is part of the innovation process. If you can create an environment where failure is not punished but expected to get to the next level, you will have less fear and more success.

As a Visionary CEO, you must have a clear vision of the organization's future and communicate it effectively. I have met many brilliant CEOs, but they are often so scattered that their people feel lost about moving forward. A compelling vision can motivate employees to embrace learning and growth.

When I started my new job as a dean, I met several times with my new boss. Every time, I asked, "What are my specific job requirements that you expect me to do weekly? For example, do I need to have reports on how many students are in the programs, our retention, and curriculum issues?" She never answered the question, leaving me to guess what I needed to do. Leaders need to set specific learning goals and expectations for employees. Encourage them to set their own development goals as well and make sure they are aligned with organizational objectives. After reviewing their job requirements, I always ask my employees, "What do you think you would want to add to this job that might be missing?"

The next step is to invest in training and development. When you have continued training and development, allocate resources for training, workshops, and courses. Provide opportunities for employees to acquire new skills and knowledge. Another important aspect is to have support mentorship and coaching programs to facilitate learning from experienced team members.

Another important aspect of innovation is to encourage risk-taking. I was encouraged to take risks growing up. Culture dictated to take the safe route. That has changed as our world of innovation of products and technology has grown. But as leaders, we need to create a safe environment for taking calculated risks. Encourage employees to step out of their comfort zones without fear of severe repercussions if they fail.

MANAGING STRESS AND MAINTAINING MENTAL WELL-BEING AS AN ENTREPRENEUR

Every person is different in how they manage stress. I thrive in stressful situations, tight deadlines, and adapting because I played sports at a high level. These are all things I had to do on the court, so they transfer well into entrepreneurship. Entrepreneurship can be incredibly rewarding, but it can also be highly stressful and demanding. These are some strategies and self-care practices I find effective.

Time management and prioritization is a big one for me. I run four companies along with many more projects. Effective time management is crucial. Entrepreneurs often wear many hats and juggle numerous responsibilities. Using time management techniques like the Eisenhower Matrix or the Pomodoro Technique can help you stay focused and reduce stress. I live and die by my Google calendar; it's essentially my personal assistant when I am on the run.

Something I am not great at is delegating and asking for help. Don't try to do everything yourself. Delegate tasks to team members or consider outsourcing certain responsibilities. Seeking advice or mentorship from experienced entrepreneurs can also be invaluable. I regularly reach out to business partners or friends in business to get their feedback.

Another tough one for me, since I work remotely, is to maintain a work-life balance. I like to work; I love my job. However, we all still need that balance. Set clear boundaries between your work and personal lives. Make time for family, friends, and hobbies. Taking regular breaks and vacations can help you recharge and prevent burnout. We plan a big vacation every summer with the kids to make sure we detach and spend quality time as a family making memories.

As a former high-level athlete, exercise and nutrition have always played a big role in my life. When I changed to business, there was a lot more sitting in front of the computer. Physical health is closely linked to mental well-being. I regularly exercise to reduce stress and boost my mood. Eating a balanced diet and staying hydrated are also essential for energy and mental clarity. I have a bad habit of drinking a lot of coffee and not enough water, so I try to keep water at my desk to remind me.

I learned about mindfulness and meditation from my coach. I thought it was a lot of hocus pocus. However, when my coach had us sit, close our eyes, and imagine hitting or blocking the volleyball, it put me in the right mindset for the game. He also taught us how practicing mindfulness and getting in the right mindset before a game or a big meeting can reduce stress and help you focus. Meditation can help you manage stress and improve focus as well. I like to go kayaking or paddle boarding and meditate and be quiet among the water and wildlife. Even a few minutes of meditation each day can significantly affect your mental well-being.

I must admit that my sleep hygiene is not great. I run a million miles a minute and don't sleep much. Unlike other people, I also can go for quite some time with little sleep. But all the studies say prioritize sleep. And despite me being a bit of a hypocrite in this, I must encourage you to be better than me. I am working on sleeping more. Lack of sleep can negatively impact decision-making and increase stress. Create a sleep-friendly environment and stick to a consistent sleep schedule.

One of my most powerful things is my network and social support. When I started, I was a bit of a loner. I felt like I didn't fit into certain groups of women. But that was the worst thing I could have done to myself. I soon learned the hard way that I needed to surround myself with a supportive network of friends, family, and fellow entrepreneurs. Sharing your challenges and successes with others who understand can provide emotional relief. I have experienced this firsthand.

Studies show that if you write your goals down, you are 90 percent more likely to accomplish those goals. You need to set realistic goals. Be realistic about what you can achieve in a given timeframe. Setting unattainable goals can lead to stress and disappointment. I like to do thirty-day, six-month, one-year, three-year, and five-year goals. This integrates immediate and long-term goals.

Organization is a big one for me. I am an organization monster. You must stay organized to minimize your stress. Use tools like calendars, to-do lists, and project management software to stay organized and reduce the mental clutter that can contribute to stress. My laundry and dishes not being done or my house being messy bothers me, too. I hired a house cleaner to come once a week and do all the deep cleaning like toilets, floors, and laundry. This lifted a big burden so I could have less stress and focus more on what I need to do for work and be a better mom.

Even though I have three degrees and a 25 and 23-year-old company, I have learned that leaders must be continuously learning. However, continuous learning does not mean traditional school. It could be getting a mentor or hanging out with people who know more than you or have more experience. Continuous learning opens you to the idea that you never can have enough training. Invest in your personal and professional development. Learning new skills and gaining knowledge can boost confidence and reduce the anxiety that often comes with uncertainty.

Finally, celebrate small wins. The other day, I was working on several things I needed others to buy in on. I received a lot of yeses. The deal is not finalized, and there is much work to do. However, I got four yeses. That was huge for me, and I celebrated. We have to find joy in the small things just as much as the big things. Entrepreneurship can be challenging, and it's easy to focus on the long-term goals. Take time to celebrate small victories along the way to maintain motivation and a positive mindset.

Remember that self-care practices can vary from person to person. Finding what works best for you and integrating these practices into your daily or weekly routine is essential. Prioritizing your mental and physical well-being is not only beneficial for you as an entrepreneur but can also contribute to the long-term success of your business.

Fostering a Sense of Curiosity and Innovation Within your Company

Fostering a sense of curiosity and innovation within a company is crucial for long-term growth and success. These are some strategies that I have used to help cultivate this mindset and how it can positively influence business growth.

One of the most important ways to create and foster a sense of innovation and curiosity is starting at the top with the leaders.

Leaders should lead by example and demonstrate a genuine interest in learning and trying new things. Encourage open communication, experimentation, and risk-taking. Celebrate both successes and failures as opportunities for learning.

Leaders often overlook the importance of investing in training for their employees and keeping it as up-to-date as possible in their industry. Regular training gives employees more confidence and encourages their ability to be more innovative. Integrating cross-functional teams encourages collaboration among employees from diverse backgrounds and skill sets. Different perspectives often lead to innovative solutions.

I have found that fun, healthy competition among your people is great. Offer incentives for innovation. Rewarding employees for innovative ideas and contributions and bringing in friendly competition is great.

Also, we don't want to forget about creating feedback loops. We must regularly gather feedback from employees, customers, and partners to refine and improve products, services, and processes.

Additionally, partnering with universities, research institutions, startups, and industry peers can help gain fresh perspectives and access to cutting-edge technology. Your network can be a very powerful aspect of innovation. Instead of remaking things, you can partner to improve your services and products.

By fostering a culture of curiosity and innovation, companies can stay ahead in competitive markets, adapt to changing conditions, and create new growth opportunities. Innovation allows organizations to explore new markets, products, and technologies, ultimately leading to sustained success.

Habits and Daily Routines that Help Maintain and Strengthen My CEO Mindset

Developing a visionary mindset and strategic thinking capabilities is essential for aspiring leaders who want to make a significant impact. Here are some things I do to help me grow and strengthen my mindset.

I recently started a very tech-savvy project. Although the project fits my skills, the tech side is a bit of a weakness. Therefore, I have attended workshops and conferences focused on this technology. I needed to learn how to use and implement it and where to buy it. Now, I have learned an entirely new mindset on tech and how to implement it. Seek out opportunities to learn from experts and gain exposure to new ideas.

Although it's not always popular, it is important to seek diverse viewpoints. This is hard for me, but different viewpoints have helped me look at things differently and have helped with my approach. Never be too proud to hear all points of view, even if some of them seem mute. Engage with people from different backgrounds and industries to challenge your assumptions. I traveled the world early in my career, and experiencing different people, cultures, and beliefs led to a more powerful mindset. It made me a better leader.

Today, when I speak with business leaders, they often complain that this younger generation doesn't know how to think strategically. They don't know how to analyze trends or stay attuned to industry trends, emerging technologies, and shifts in the business landscape. They have book knowledge but no experience to guide them. I have found that experience—good or bad—is the most important and powerful aspect of keeping a visionary mindset. Do what you can to get as much experience as possible.

I always remember the story of Blockbuster and Netflix, and I got to live it when it was all happening. Netflix started with Redbox, where you could rent a movie from one of the box locations. Then, they got into something new and powerful—streaming. No one knew the power of streaming, but Blockbuster did not attempt to compete with their competitors or try something different. They underestimated their competitors and lacked innovation, leading to their demise and eventually bankruptcy. Today, everything is streaming. As a leader, even if it seems far-fetched, you need to embrace innovation. Foster a culture of innovation. Encourage your team to generate and explore new ideas. Be open to change. Embrace innovation and be willing to adapt your strategies as circumstances evolve.

Another aspect that has made my companies strong competitors is I built a strong team. I knew several good people I worked with at previous companies who I loved to work with, and they knew their stuff. I took the best of the best and offered them all jobs. They gladly accepted because they loved working with and for me. I found people I didn't have to micromanage; they were innovative and willing to learn and grow. They weren't driven by their egos. This has kept my company at the forefront of what we do and continue to do because I keep bringing in strong team members.

I have found, especially after Covid, that resilience is an important aspect of any leader or company. Covid nearly destroyed my company. I had to have so much grit, courage, and resilience to get them back to where they were before the shutdowns. Part of resilience is accepting setbacks. They happen in every business. I always tell young entrepreneurs that if your account has not been in the negative, you're not a real entrepreneur. Setbacks happen all the time, but it's our resilience that keeps us and our vision going. Understand that not every strategic move will lead to immediate success. Learn from failures and setbacks. It's the failures that create success.

Be self-aware. Nothing is more frustrating to me than when someone has no clue how their behavior and actions affect others. An example is someone who is always late to everything. It drives me bonkers. If I can get there on time while managing four companies, kids, and life, you can, too. However, those people often seem blind to their behaviors and actions. Reflect on your strengths and weaknesses and understand your leadership style and areas for improvement. You can't be a visionary CEO if you don't know your weaknesses and how to combat them.

Developing a visionary mindset and strategic thinking capabilities is an ongoing journey. It requires a commitment to learning, adaptability, and a willingness to take risks. You can become a more effective and influential leader in your field by continuously honing these skills and staying focused on your long-term goals.

About the Author

Dr. Julie Ducharme is a sought-after keynote speaker, author, business consultant, entrepreneur, instructor, and special consultant in women's empowerment. She is the creator, founder, and CEO of Julie's Party People, JD Consulting, Synergy Learning, and Taylor Elite Sports.